Kleptocracy African Style

by

Alex Eke

Dorrance Publishing Co
585 Alpha Drive
Pittsburgh, PA 15238
Visit our website at *www.dorrancebookstore.com*

ISBN: 978-1-4809-4155-7
eISBN: 978-1-4809-4178-6

Prologue

The views expressed are solely from compilations of newspaper articles and scholarly journals from the individual countries mentioned and by brave journalists as they told the stories that impacted the countries where they live, work and raise their children and sometimes at the risk of death. It must be understood that print media can be bias for or against a particular leader, but it should be seen in its totality.

When you look around the African continent, you will see children with ascites; Kwashiorkor blotted leg and visibly numbered ribs, some with runny nose, gazing perpetually into the horizon, beckoning the gods for a change in fortune, asking when this tribulation will be over. The hunger pain makes it feel like your rib muscles are fused to the rib, making each breath a labor for life. The nights seem like eternity, you toss and turn, and at last, day light. Not a moment too soon. Only to relive the nightmare. Their misfortunes are brought about by the corruption of those elected to care for their needs and protect their future. Where the future of Liberian children is not zero but negative, their leaders can afford to send their children to schools England, Unites States of America, Canada, and Germany.

Africa must rise as one to fight the injustice crippling the continent.

Alex Eke

This manuscript is dedicated to the brave journalists risking their lives to make sure the story is told.

To my beautiful wife, Gladys, and my wonderful children—Grace, Blessing, Theophilus and Faith—for their steadfast support and love.

Africa is a beautiful continent, made up of fifty-four countries richly endowed with vast natural resources. This quilt that is African continent is stitched together by languages, cultures and tribes that are lush in tradition. Embedded in this treasure of traditions is an incestuous relationship of African leadership with corruption on a massive scale. On the other hand, African leaders must escape the perception that African leaders are corrupt and the nations that make up the African continent are mismanaged. The Africans have been looking at what they are willing to tolerate and what they are tolerating is their leaders stealing the countries resources away from Africans.

The angle offered in this record is not exhaustive of all there are to be discussed concerning corruption and political leadership in the continent of Africa, but particularly Nigeria, which boasts of the largest economy and population in Africa and the world's eighth largest exporter of crude oil. This content will only approach the subject matter of corrupt leadership from the perspective of this degeneracy's contributions to public policy failures and its implications to socio-economic development of the African continent.

Bribery is taking money to give people preferential treatment. Officials accepting bribes to move people up on the housing waiting list. Stealing money or resources that are supposed to be under government control, using public money to buy personal goods like a car, houses and airline ticket is embezzlement. Making false claims for benefits is Fraud. African institutions and leaders are engaged in Extortion: a public official forcing someone to give them benefits in exchange for acting or not acting in a particular way. Police officer, taking money from criminals to lose their case evidence. All of these vices are happening in African nations simultaneously. It is from this prism that we will look at corruption in Africa with its magnitude in insecurity and regression.

The human rights atrocities committed by some African leaders are beyond the scope of this manuscript.

Chapter 1

The axiom that history repeats itself has a more worrisome meaning in Africa's political and leadership discourse. Corrupt politicians and prostitution have existed since antiquity as one of the worse and at the same time, most widespread forms of corrupt behaviors in continental Africa. Both acts are disadvantageous to the administration of public affair. In Africa, laws and regulations are influenced to suit certain individual interests that are separate from society concern.[1] There is no democracy without legal dispensation, responsibility and representation, Africa must not be the exception. Africa must repudiate the characterization of weak institutions and leadership, ineffective bureaucracy, a weak judicial system, lack of respect for the rule of law, debilitating corruption, a weak security system, a decaying social and economic infrastructure, as well as a timid and weak private sector.

The period leading to 1960 saw many African countries gaining independence from the colonial masters such as Britain, Spain, Portugal, France, and Denmark. All of Africa's emancipated countries were lacking the experience of selfless governance. During this period, paying and receiving bribes, fraud, embezzlement, self-dealing, and conflicts of interest were the primary sources for creating wealth and all too common; thus, these became the incentives for public service. This was also a period where core elite, educated minority had a disproportionate influence on state policies and resources, leading to outright economic collapse in many African countries. Unequivocally, bribery was extremely high. The system, if there was any, was riddled with special interest or sweetheart deals that favored only those in and close to power over the majority of African people. The restricted access to the decision-making process limited the space for civil society participation in governance processes and created over-concentration of power in the hands of very few. This bred corruption. The consequence was a high level of resentment toward the ruling elite, which in part led to the bloody military coup and revolutions of 1960's and its initial support amongst the people. This is the foremost reason given for regime change in Nigeria, Ghana, Liberia, Guinea Egypt and Libya. But, the ordinary African citizen quickly realized that he may have been better off in the European and white man's government; at least the levels of corruption were not excessive and there were check and balances with these administrators answerable to their parent nations. The military and successive governments however failed to correct the mischiefs and the problems were magnified.[2] It is said that corruption and Africa is like conjoined twin, and it is a destructive relationship that benefits no one. One cannot discuss Africa without the corresponding corruption ravaging the continent. "It has been the inaction of those who could have acted, the indifference of those who should have known and the silence of the voice of justice when it mattered most that has made it possible for evil to triumph. In other words bad things happen when good men do nothing."[3]

The Commanding General Officer of Fort Leonard Wood, Army Installation, Missouri, whose command and operational philosophy is Mission First, People Always and Team of Teams. [4] This philosophy is deceptively simple. For the African leaders, the **mission** is protecting the country from enemies within and outside of the nation's territorial boundaries, tackling dilapidated infrastructure, crime, security, high level of unemployment, hunger and literacy. **People always,** taking care of those you are charged to lead, and their prosperity and happiness. Immediate reconciliation of discord by clear and direct communication to promote **Team of Teams**, an impressive team of superb men and women of uprightness, operating with dignity, respect and trust in common purpose and destiny that binds the nation together. Create a shared consciousness with the nation by assembling the best minds in the country irrespective of tribe or ethnicity, to achieve optimal decision making, working in unison to achieve goals greater than the individual. A team with undistracted effort, great imagination and devotion. A team that represents the entire country advancing in consonance. In the African continent, advancing in consonance means like-minded individual stealing what is not bolted down; it is each leader for himself. This fleecing of the continent has been turned into an art by some African leaders.

According to the US Army Ethics Regulation, any Solicitation and acceptance of a gift becomes a bribe when it's given in exchange for official action. In Africa, this exchange or compensation for official action appears to be the norm, not just an occasional or arduous exception.

Africa is a continent blessed with many mineral resources, still more than seventy percent of its population live on just a little over one dollar a day as a result of corruption and economic mismanagement. The rich in Africa are fabulously wealthy and the poor only survive on one meal a day and grace of God.

Most of the nations in Africa achieved independence with Singapore and Malaysia but are incomparable to the industrial base, output and quality of life advancements of the later. It is postulated that Nigeria donated oil palm seed to Malaysia, but Malaysia is now the leading producer of palm oil in the world. It is difficult to understand how good men could stand by and allows their country to be pillaged; slavery, this time, has nothing to do with the exploitation of the African continent today, but marginalization of youth, women and the mismanagement of national resources contribute to stark inequalities in the distribution of wealth, income and benefits. In essence, African leaders are economically and politically enslaving their own citizens.

John Kennedy said, "Don't ask what your country can do for you but what you can do to advance the progress of your nation." JFK's statement has become a political catch phrase in the African continent. The African leaders are indeed asking what they can do for their country alright, and the answer is pillage and embezzle the treasury of the nation into dark ages. The political leadership in Africa really is not the pursuit of national goal but of self-service mired in selfish interests of the elected, dictatorial or self-appointed, presumed leaders that gained power at the point of coup d'état, election manipulation and guerrilla tactics, all at the detriment of national interest. In the process, massive amount of money is looted by these so-called leaders, leaving the continent and its inhabitants impoverished. The kinds of corruptions going on in Africa has become competitive, each leader checking to see who steals the most without being apprehended, sometimes with boastful glee.

Personal aggrandizement, self-glorification and corruption at all levels of the society have become the end result. It is only in Nigeria and other African Countries that an Army Officer with modest income can buy a 1.5 million-dollar house in Dubai as it is alleged the Nigerian Chief of Army Staff LTG Buratai did, in his wife's name and little questions asked.[5] How can this Army officer with modest means able to service the interest on this mortgage in one of the most expensive real estate markets in the world? The Chief of Army Staff denies the allegation.

Selfless political leadership is not part of the vocabulary or lexicon of African leaders. In Africa, leaders cannot comprehend a common sight picture in battling greed and other excesses. Those that enter politics, joined for material gain. The root of the African Problem is the unwillingness and inability of its leaders to rise to their responsibility, to the challenge of personal example, which is the hallmark of true leadership. [6] The African leader in the public service seeks to further his own, his family and friends financial interest. A modest exception to this is may be the former president of Nigeria, Gen. Obasanjo Olusegun and the former President of South Africa, Nelson Mandela.

Africa is used to in-your-face corruption where police officer demands "tea" in public offices. It's almost acceptable to "buy lunch" or "see me or what can you do for me"—all of which, a euphemism for bribery. Sometimes people out rightly give a clear figure of the sum of money they want as inducement.[7] The indigenes of Africa recognize this fact, and yet they indulge to facilitate their personal and selfish business venture. This practice in the long run will leave some of them worse off than when they started because the business for which they paid the bribe will be granted to someone else who paid a bigger bribe.

In Africa, pandemic corruption, depraved governance, lack of sensitivity to civic responsibilities, ethnic violence and patronage are basic tools of the trade of politics, if you lose power; there is a serious likelihood that you may also lose your life, imprisonment or exile, perhaps a wave of ethnic cleansing or genocide against the ruling ethnic group similar to what happened in Rwanda and Burundi.

The vast mineral wealth of Africa has been crippled by corruption, inefficiency, political instability, insecurity, poverty, disease, dilapidated infrastructure and ignorance thus high levels of corruption produce an unequal distribution in income. This turns into a vicious circle. When ordinary citizens inquire about these affluences and how these government officials are able to live such an affluent and ostentatious life with their families, the familiar responses has always been, "it is not your business to inquire" or "a colleague, a good friend paid for it." No one has informed Ghanaians, Kenyans or the

Nigerians etc. who these benevolent benefactors are and why these seraphim should donate so generously, millions of dollars to fund the rich life style of dependents of the government officials outside or inside the nation.

The most unfortunate thing is these leaders use their position to pave the way for their family members to assume power upon their demise. To illustrate, Teodoro Obiang Nguoma of Equatorial Guinea, his son, Obiang Manue, is the vice president and defense minister, and Gebrial Mbega Obiang Lima, a brother from another mother, is the oil minister. His brother-in-law, Candidio Nsue Okomo, is the managing director of the state-owned oil company. African countries should not be managed like a mafia organization.

These are no leaders but demagogues, who appeal to popular aspirations and biases rather than using rational conviction or following through self-prescribed conviction to obtain the vote and true confidence of their citizens.

These national leaders pose a threat to their country because they are subject to blackmail by any individual with advanced knowledge, criminal organization and other countries. This clarion call should be considered a national security emergency and national security threat for all the counties in Africa. Which Africa are the current leaders willing to bestow their heirs? Africa cannot be more of the same. A truly public-spirited person should accept public office not for what he can get for himself — such as the profit and glamour of office — but for the opportunity which it offers him of serving his people to the best of his ability, by promoting their welfare and happiness.[8]

Chapter 2

West Africa

General Buhari, the former Head of State, after several attempts, was elected the president of **Nigeria** in 2015. He is being cogitated as the savior of Nigeria because he has taken a strong stance against corruption. Machiavelli in *The Prince* said that "it is better to be loved and feared at the same time but if you cannot have both, it is better to be feared but do not despised or alienate your subjects". General Buhari and his former henchman, Brigadier Tunde Idiagbon, disciplined by fear and alienated most Nigerians during his military regime. But the level of indiscipline during Buhari's military decree was dramatically and significantly reduced. Nigeria seems to be yearning for such a return, yet unwilling to disavow bribery and corruption.

Nigeria gained its independence from Great Britain on 1 October 1960 after a considerable and consolidated effort from some notable Nigerians Corruption in **Nigeria** started almost immediately following independence. These founding fathers of the country and The First Republic under the leadership of Sir Abubakar Tafawa Balewa, the Prime Minister, and Nnamdi Azikwe, the President, were marked by widespread corruption. Government officials looted public funds with impunity. Federal Representative and Ministers flaunted their wealth with reckless abandon. The overthrow of this regime and the assassination of the Prime Minister Balewa and other prominent Northern Nigerian leadership by LT COL Nzegwu, Kaduna ultimately initiated the serial coup that led Nigeria to disintegration, a civil war that caused almost a million lives and nearly partitioned Nigeria into southern eastern states of Biafra and Nigeria, leading to thirty-eight years of corrupt military rule. The consequence of this is still being felt by Nigerian, especially the Igbos. The most an Igbo person has risen to the highest office in Nigeria is Vice president in 1980, Alex Ekwueme. and Admiral Ebitu Ukaiwe during the military regime of GEN Babangida. Igbo ranks have been decimated in the military. This was an area where the Igbos dominated.

It was in an inquiry commissioned by the late General J. T. U. Aguiyi Ironsi—the first General Officer in Nigerian military who was sadly assassinated 194 days into the job by a group led by GEN Murtala Mohammed, with direct participation by the current President Buhari—discovered that parastatals in the previous administration of Sir, Tafawa Balewa, (especially) the Nigeria Railway Corporation, Nigeria Ports Authority, and the defunct Electricity Corporation of Nigeria and Nigeria Airways, and revealed that a number of ministers formed companies and used their influence to secure public contracts in pseudonym. This blatant cronyism and nepotism is still happening at the present time. Moreover, they were found guilty of misappropriation of funds as well as disregarding standing procedures in the award of contracts by parastatal organizations under their ministries.[9]

The Coker Commission of Inquiry in 1962, found Chief Obafemi Awolowo, the first Premier of the Western Region, guilty of corruption due in part to his failure to adhere to the standards of conduct, which were required of persons holding public office, a loan of £6.7 million was made to the Western Region government-owned National Investment and Properties Co. Ltd. for building projects out of which only £500,000 was repaid.[10] Were a US government official be involved in a series of transactions the result of which public funds were used to support an otherwise shaky financial venture in which he has direct financial interest, such government official would be forced to leave public office. But Obafemi Awolowo never repaid the rest of the loan. Nevertheless Awolowo, went on to become a revered national leader in Yoruba land and the nation of Nigeria.

The first attempt by the military to purge itself of corrupt elements occurred when General Murtala Mohammed military-led regime instituted a probe of all the military governors who served in the former Head of State, General Yakubu Gowon's administration. General Murtala Mohammed or the coup plotters main reason for the bloodless overthrow of General Gowan was failure to meet the expectations of Nigerians and reneging on return of power to civilian authority. The principle architect of this revolution was COL Joe Garba. All but two state governors were found guilty of corrupt self-enrichment in GEN Gowan's administration. In addition to seizure of some of their known properties, the officers also lost their military ranks and many were summarily discharged from the Service.[11] Murtala Mohammed came to power on a promising note, eagerness to dispense; he was taken out of power when his acclaim was loudest. His low profile and lack of ostentatious style to governance, zero approval for graft, lack of tolerance for ineptitude, permissiveness and indulgence earned him admiration of many Nigerians and malcontent of some junior officers in Nigerian Army who quickly sought and dispatch him 189 days after taking office. The desire of the coup plotters was to re-instate GEN Gowan to power may have led the assassination of Gen Mohammed. But Gen Mohammed's refusal of heavily-armed security details correspondingly led to his eventual demise. The presidents of other African countries modified their security package to travel in heavy security convoys. Even state and local government and other elected officials have adopted strict security details not so much for security reasons but to announce to the public of their approach and where about.

In 1980, General Olusegun Obasanjo, became the military head of state of Nigeria and by default beneficiary of the assassination of General Murtala Mohammed. He handed the government over to the civilian and popularly elected government of President Shehu Shagari, against the advice of so many African military heads of states.[12] This marked a brief end to military government in Nigeria but gave rise to resurgence in corruption. It was claimed that over $16 billion in oil revenues were unaccounted for between 1979 and 1983 during the reign of President Shehu Shagari and no single infrastructural development was accomplished. During this period, federal government buildings would mysteriously go up in flames, most especially just before the onset of ordered audits of government accounts of the ministries, making it impossible to discover written evidence of embezzlement and fraud. It must be realized that this was before the era of computer back-ups, redundant files and forensic accounting. No politician symbolized the graft and avarice under Shagari's government more than his combative Transport Minister, Alhaji Umaru Dikko. The escapade played out at Heathrow International Airport in London in 1982, under the direction of the then head of state GEN Buhari, who paid Israeli security agents to kidnap Dikko off the street of London, incapacitated

Dikko with a powerful anesthetic drug which rendered him semi-conscious, and attempted to smuggle him back to Nigeria in a crate marked diplomatic content. He was a diplomatic content alright. Save for the astute observation of a cargo handler. This fiasco fractured diplomatic relations between Nigeria and Great Britain. Had Dikko been sent back to Nigeria under the prevailing condition, he would have faced an uncertain and untimely death under the hands of the bellicose and contentious Gen Tunde Idiagbon and General Buhari, his boss. Umaru Dikko was alleged to have mismanaged about 4 billion in public funds meant for the importation of rice. [13] General Buhari promised to bring corrupt officials and their agents to account for this mismanagement. However, Buhari was himself unceremoniously toppled by General Ibrahim Babangida, his Chief of Army Staff, in a bloodless in-house coup on 27 August 1985. Buhari, who has not shown mercy to the military even in his ongoing anti-corruption war, the coup d'état, led by former military president, General Ibrahim Babangida and General Aliyu Gusau, removed Buhari, in August 1985, to save themselves from his wrath. This was corroborated by President Obasanjo in his book, *My Watch: Now and Then*. But why did the then President Obasanjo, knowing what he knew now, make Aliyu Gassau his National Security Adviser and T.Y. Danjuma Defense Minister? This is a shrewd political maneuvering by Obasanjo, knowing that these individuals still have powerful connections in the military. Maybe with these individuals close, this may prevent another coup. This is the old adage; keep your friends close but your enemies closer. Buhari, in trying to achieve his desired goal of maintaining strict financial discipline and accountability, ruled the Nigerians from 1983 to 1985, suspiciously imprisoning corrupt politicians while transmitting draconian orders to check leadership excesses. The fissure in his leadership style was the misguided conceptualization that the primary purpose of his administration is for the imprisonment of society activists and detractors of his government like the former Soviet Union or North Korea.[14] This was the first time drug traffickers, convicted by military tribunal, were publicly executed by firing squad in Nigeria. The next thirteen years following Babangida's regime in Nigeria saw no serious attempt to stop corruption and to some extent, was encouraged. Meanwhile, corruption reached an alarming rate and became institutionalized during Babangida's regime.[15] In 1994, The Okigbo Panel Report on the Reorganization and Reform of the Central Bank of Nigeria indicted former Military President, General Ibrahim Badamosi Babangida, former

Head of State, late General Sani Abacha, and former Governor of the Central Bank of Nigeria, the late Alhaji Abdulkadir Ahmed, for mismanaging about $12.4 billion oil windfall between 1988 and 1994. The word "mismanagement" used in this report is generous, the word that should have been used is "fleeced the Nigerian nation and citizens". A summary of the panel's report submitted to the Federal Government revealed that General Ibrahim Babangida's regime connived with the leadership of the Central Bank of Nigeria to squander the entire fortune on unproductive or dubious projects. General Babangida's nickname was "Maradona" after the famous Argentine mid-fielder's fancy foot work and dribbler for his selective manipulation of the truth. Babangida was later ousted from power by another military strongman under the leadership of General Sani Abacha on 17 November 1993 a protégé and his Chief of Army Staff. Abacha's regime only furthered the deep-seated corrupt practices of which, he is the chief architect. Under General Abacha, corrupt practices became blatant, systematic and legendary. President Obasanjo describes Gen Abacha as an Indian giver, a do "gooder," who fixes a meal for a sightless man and as soon as his visitors glanced away, he nicks the pot of soup and spoon from the blind man for himself.[16] General Abacha, his family, alongside his associates and cronies looted Nigeria's coffers with casual intemperance. The extent of Abacha's venality seemed to have surpassed that of other notorious African rulers such as Mobutu Sese Seku of Congo. General Sani Abacha, Nigeria's former Head of State and Commander-in-Chief were discovered to have stolen over $3.0 billion which were found in foreign bank accounts.

The end result is, Nigeria became a hostage in the hands of the elite military class with various high ranking military officers, at distinct times, seizing power or attempting to seize power primarily to enrich self not to improve the lives of fellow Nigerian citizens.

Tafa Balogun, a former Inspector General of Police under President Olusegun Obasanjo was found guilty of diverting N17.0 billion. This is akin to the Director of the Federal Bureau of Investigation in US embezzling 100 million dollars of the organization's fund. The direct implication was that the salaries and other benefits to the Nigerian Police Force were paid several months late. He only spent six months in jail with some known assets confiscated.

In an attempt to meet their family and social obligations, the police officers resorted to a life of corruption, bribery and in most cases, armed robberies and contract killing. Nigerian Police Force has been implicated in extrajudicial killings, armed robberies, intimidation, and false imprisonment. Under the military, the police gradually deteriorated. It became plausible to cite them for the most hideous to the most frivolous acts that violate the rights of the very Nigerian citizens whose friend they purported to be. Thus, was born the process which led to the police becoming a highly corrupt institution with its officers not only commercializing the process of law enforcement but also taking pride in doing so, in fact, often defiantly making a public show of extorting money from those perceived as having fallen afoul of the law.

It appears that the Police, who were supposed to enforce the law, began increasingly to operate outside the confines of the law, and therefore building and promoting legacies of inefficiency, illegality and decadence. The management of the police pension scheme has recently revealed a leadership that was grossly insensitive. It becomes very appalling to hear that over N200 million (two hundred million naira) would be spent to verify less than twenty police pensioners overseas. The question is what then would be the total pension of those retired officers when over two hundred million is spent to verify them. Some of the state officials involved in this scam have come under prosecution by the EFCC. Esai Dangaba, Atiku Kigo, Ahmed Inuwa Wada, John Yusufu, Veronica Ulonma, and Zani Zira were prosecuted for defrauding the police pension scheme in the sum of N32.8 billion.

Immigration and Custom Services received some negative ratings by all groups of concerned stakeholders. Observers considered this negative image an off shoot of the lingering legacy of protracted military rule, during which period, several societal institutions were effectively nullified, resulting in what some concerned patrons referred to as a "vandalization" of the structure and normal procedures for purposeful public sector management.[17] Non-state institutions and civil society groups are too weak, and therefore unable to put the national institutions in check.[18] According to Nuhu Ribadu, who incidentally was almost poisoned for fighting fraud said corruption has taken over as the engine of the Nigerian society and replaced the rule of law".[19] David Cameron has described Nigeria and Afghanistan as "fantastically corrupt" in a conversation with the Queen as reported by BBC. "Mo Ibrahim said that Nigeria is a failure in good governance."[20] With such statement, how far is Nigeria from a failed state?

In a country that is seeking foreign loan forgiveness, it is unfathomable to think that a country such as Nigeria, rich in oil resources has massive unemployment and constant disruption in electricity delivery to the households and businesses, Nigeria would import refined oil at huge expense while exporting crude oil. The local oil refineries are inadequate at producing sufficient quantity of oil for local consumption. The refineries are constantly in disrepair due to poor maintenance. In spite of huge sums involved the turn-around, maintenance of the oil refineries and gas turbines, to position the country to energy efficiency have not resulted in an inefficient performance of the oil refineries; and yet Nigeria imports refined oil sometimes creating fuel shortage and scarcity all over the nation especially during peak travel season such as December period when most Nigerian Christians travel to their village to see friends and family. This is a period of felicity and visitation.

During president Obasanjo's era, he invited Shell Oil Company with fifty-one percent share in the Nigerian oil refinery but Shell Oil Company turned him down for the following reasons: the capacity of oil refinery production is too low, the poor state of maintenance and repair of the refineries in spite of the fees paid for turn-around maintenance. Shell Oil Company prefers upstream and deep ocean oil exploration than the bureaucratic tangle and corruption in the Nigerian system. Shell Oil Company should be commended for their courage to steer clear of Nigerian corruption but they did a dis-service to Nigerians by abandoning a venture, although not so profitable to Shell Oil Company, and would have reduced the dependency of Nigerians from fuel refined abroad.

The selfish reasons of the perpetrators prevent the public from the attainment of optimum benefits of public policy.

Nigeria is a nation that pays its legislators a combined total of a little over 500 members more than most of its thirty-six States' budget. Nigerian legislators are the highest paid elected government workers in the world. For example 109 senators and 360 members of the House of Representatives gulp as much as N120 billion in a year. At the current exchange rate, it is about 70 billion US dollars. This is twice the 2015 budget of Ekiti State of N80.774 billion, a state with the population of 2,384,212 people. How equitable is it for less than 500 national legislators to spend N120 billions annually when Osun State with population of 3,423,535 people and the unfunded 2015 Appropriation Bill of N201 billion is yet to pay its employees' salaries for seven months? Benue State has as many as 4,219,244 people, it budgeted N98.54 billion; Zamfara has 3,259,846 citizens and budgeted N92.80 billion; and Ebonyi budgeted N80.02 billion for 2,173,501 people.

The total budgets of these three states is half of the National Assembly's. This is an illegal and unconstitutional concentration of scarce national resources in the hands of the legislators and executive office holders that must be reversed. For instance, Kano State budgeted N210 billion in 2015. It has 9,383,682 people. The budget per capita of Kano, estimated at N22, 379 is miserable compared to the budget per capita of the National Assembly at N293, 398,533. While the ordinary Nigerian living—in Dutsa in a small single room in a wretched slum which has neither an in-door bathroom, kitchen, clean water, nor electricity, and no road—yet the legislators have the dispensation to request a raise in their salary. No country can prosper or sustain this widening gap in resource allocation between the governed and some elected government officials. There is agitation in the national assembly to increase these legislators' salary.[21] The indications are that our corruption has become legendary, with leadership at home and away, says President Obasanjo in *My Watch Now and Then*. He continues, we hear of government officials demanding billions in naira, judiciary demanding dollars in millions and legislatures turning oversight functions over to extortion in addition to cover-up, corruption and kickbacks. National Assembly's annual budget is shrouded leading to Nigerian tax payers maintaining a senator with over 300 million Naira, and in the lower House, with over 200 million while many millions of Nigerians make less than 100 naira a day. [22] The brand of corruption in Nigeria transcends the stealing of public fund and stashing million or billions. It is also in the level of wages these legislatures allot to themselves. According to Judge Ajibola, the Central Bank of Nigeria estimates that about twenty-five percent of recurrent budget expenditure goes to political class and its connections.[23] How can a nation sustain such excesses?

It will take an average Nigerian worker 1,638 years to earn the yearly salary of a Nigerian Senator which is estimated to be $189,500 base salary. It has been reported that the Nigerian legislature approved the purchase of 108 SUV's for the members at the cost of 35 million Naira when the actual price of these vehicles is closer to 7 million Naira per vehicle. This is 500 percent cost of the vehicles. Realize that they are already receiving transportation allowance as part of their pay package. In defense of this excess, a representative member quipped, "Do you want us to trek to work?" With such salary, you might as well fly to work. They also approved a loan for the legislatures to purchase the same vehicle. This is double dipping at the expense of Nigerians.

The Nigerian National Assembly has lapsed into all sorts of misconduct and corruption. Efforts at self-discipline or monitoring have been perfunctory ending in cover-up. And reversal of sanctions previously prescribed against errant members.[24] This is a period when Nigeria is experiencing financial difficulty and a shortage of fuel.

It is only in Nigeria that an elected Senator Buruji Kashamu, representing Ogun State East senatorial zone, indicted for drug trafficking in Chicago is seeking the governments help from being extradited to the USA. If he is innocent of the charges, the State Department and US Embassy in Lagos will gladly give him the visa to enter the USA and respond to the charges against him. "Orange is the new black" television series is based on the account of his escapade as a drug mogul before he absconded and hiding in plain sight, in Nigeria. His accomplice, Piper Chapman, has been convicted and spent time in jail. It is postulated that with the increasing incidence of fraud and fraudulent activities in Nigeria, corruption is gradually becoming a normal way of life.[25] Financial irregularities have permeated the business as well as private sector and the extent of this fraud is commensurate with the perpetrators capacity and official position. The chronicles of high-profile list of corruption in Nigeria to include the arraignment of a one-time governor of Kogi State, Kwara State, Delta State by the Economic and Financial Crimes Commission (EFCC)—the premiere watchdog for economic crimes for embezzling and defrauding the state to the tune of N4 billion. In September 2006, the EFCC had thirty-one of Nigeria's thirty-six state governors under investigation for corruption. It does not mean that the rest were innocent. A one-time female Senator from Ogun State was quizzed by EFCC for receiving $100,000 stolen from the Ministry of Health. The Health Minister and her deputy were questioned for stealing over N30 million from the Ministry's unspent funds from the previous year. The oil subsidy and the police pension scam are the latest manifestations of wanton corruption traceable to attitudinal recklessness of Nigerian leadership. So far, the EFCC has docked twenty of those who defrauded the federation through the fuel subsidy fund. Some of the cases revealed included Ogunbambo, Theck and Fargo swindled the federal government of over N976 million for fuel they did not supply. Taylor, Nasaman and Ali were involved in N4.4billion fraud, and Alao was docked for N2.6-billion scam. Tukur, Ochonogo, External Oil, collectively defrauded the state to the sum of N1.899 billion. Nadabo, Peters and Abalaka and Pacific Silver stole the sum of N1.464

billion and Watgbasoma, Ugo-Ngadi, Ebenezer, Ejidele and Ontario Oil defrauded the Federal Government of Nigeria to the tune of N1.959 billion.

Of the nine collapsed commercial banks in Nigeria, about one trillion naira was reported to have been lost through different financial malpractices. The highest fraud ever reported in any particular year by a Nigerian bank occurred in 1998 when United Bank for Africa plc wrote off N786m on account of fraud. **First Bank of Nigeria Limited**, **Guaranty Trust Bank Plc** (GT-Bank), **Zenith Bank Plc**, United Bank for Africa Plc (UBA), Access Bank Plc, Skye Bank Plc, Ecobank Nigeria and Diamond Bank Plc have been designated by the Central Bank of Nigeria (CBN) as "too big to fail", owing to the fact that their failure could pose a systemic risk to the banking industry and the economy at large. The eight banks alone account for seventy-five per-cent of the banking sector in terms of earnings, profitability assets, customer deposits and branch networks. The former directors of the failed banks collectively owed the failed banks N53.3 billion out of which the Nigeria Deposit Insurance Corporation (NDIC) has so far recovered a paltry N4.722 billion. The scope and scale of fraud in the Nigerian banking industry is not surprising, given the profile of Nigeria as a corrupt and fraudulent nation.[26]

Debtors to Failed Banks:

Adeyeba Adekunle Johns N7b (Gulf Bank)
Alhaji Sanusi Ado Bayero N45.003 million
Babajide Rogers N11.874 million
Muyiwa Osho N242.1 million
Ebitimi Banigo N3.2b with N10 million recovered (All States Trust Bank)
Professor Nta Henshaw N17.9 million
Alh I.Aminu Saleh & A. Aminu Saleh - N26.918 million (Eagle Bank)
Paul Achimugu - N5.5 million
Alh K.A. Olatunde N13.3 million (Trade Bank)
Alh S.Y.Abdullahi N1.25bn
Alh Sha'aba Lafiagi N1.156 million
David Chuka Nwosu N3.4 million
Prince S. Adedoyin & Mrs. Sola Adeoti
N5.584b with N453 million recovered (City Express Bank)
Angela Onyeador N30.7 million (Assurance Bank of Nigeria plc)

Chuka Nwokoko N31.9 million
Moore Onyekaba N3.6 million
Sir Emeka Ofor- N7.5bn with N3.8bn recovered (African Express Bank)
Chief Victor Odili N54.3 million (Liberty Bank)
Dr. T.C. Osanakpo - N43.6 million
Alh B.I. Bunu, Chief F.EC. Adiele, Chief Jude Akpunku, Dr. Sam Eke, Nnamdi Anyaehie, Nze Maduako N9.3bn (Hallmark Bank)
J.I. Abulime - N5.8 million (Lead Bank)
Mallam Saleh Jambo - N17.2 million
Captain Onu & Chief D. Onyia N26.6 million
Sen Chris Adighije N1.9 million (Metropolitan Bank)
Sen Mike Ajaegbo - N210 million
Chief (Mrs.) R. Adiukwu-Bakare over N1.093 billion
Great Ogboru - N799.7 million
Oladapo Sarumi - N3.8 million
Chief S.O. Bakare - N800 million.[27]

To put these into perspective, 1 US dollar is equal to 150 Nigerian naira in 2009 exchange rate. Other components of fraud include bribes cronyism, nepotism, in-appropriate political donation, kickbacks, artificial pricing and frauds of all kinds, and amounts as a quid pro quo. **"Scratch my back and I will scratch your back"**. Violence, criminal and illicit activities are committed with the objective of earning wealth rapidly, illegally in a manner that violates existing legislation and these include narcotic drug trafficking, money laundering, embezzlement, bribery, looting and child labor. Illegal oil bunkering and illegal mining, tax evasion, foreign exchange malpractice (including counterfeiting of currency, theft of intellectual property, sea piracy, open market abuse, dumping of toxic waste, obstruction of justice, kidnapping for ransom) has become a profession in Nigeria and dealing in prohibited goods, committed under the watchful eyes of Customs and Immigration Services and the Police, and all those tasked to protect the nation.[28]

These frauds usually involve a complex web of conspiracy and deception that often mask the actual cause.[29] A survey by Transparency International, a German based international organization that interviewed business people worldwide, listed Nigeria as the second out of one hundred and forty-six nation's most corrupt country in the world.[30]

The Independent Corrupt Practices and Other-Related Offences Commission will arraign a member of the House of Representatives, Farouk Lawan, on a seven-count charge bearing on corrupt enrichment. The charge stems from allegations by a businessman, Chief Femi Otedola, that Lawan demanded and received $620,000 as a bribe from him while he (Lawan) was the chairman of the House AdHoc Committee on Monitoring of Fuel Subsidy Regime.

The level of corruption is a serious concern and remains the greatest challenge to Nigeria and the African continent. The majority of Nigerians are yet to buy into the anti-corruption program of the Federal Government, particularly at the state and local government levels. The consequences of the endemic corruption continue to impede development and threaten security and lives of the citizenry. Poverty, unemployment, insecurity of life and property and decaying infrastructure are the common features which are largely attributable to the high incidence of corruption. This has reached an unbridled level. The total absence of control as everything is ready for grab at various levels has dire consequences for the society. Road construction contract award where the minister and the civil servants at various levels take bribes or shake down the contractors result in poor quality work delivered. Health care sector fraud involving hospitals, pharmaceutical departments and unexecuted contracts for provision of infrastructure are all avenues through which public funds are illegally diverted, sometimes in collaboration with vendors of outsourced services in the delivery of substandard products including drugs.[31] The scale and magnitude of the corruption seen in Nigeria is an outgrowth of weak social values, which manifests in greed and moral decadence. Former Governor of Bayelsa State Diepreye Alamieyeseigha, who absconded and later tried to re-enter Nigeria from London dressed as a woman through the back waters of Nigerian, was convicted for misappropriation of the state's fund and later pardoned by the former President Goodluck Jonathan saying "the whole thing is about self-interest".[32] President Obasanjo wrote that an American friend of his said that "corruption in Nigeria has assumed great proportions and is in the bed room of your president".[33] General Sani Abacha, who took the helms of Nigerian leadership after a coup, became a billionaire. Upon his death in 1998, the Nigerian government uncovered over 3 billion dollars linked to this sadistic despot, held in private and proxy bank accounts in Switzerland, Luxembourg and Liechtenstein. Following a series of negotiations between the Abacha family and the government of Nigeria, Abacha's son Mohammed eventually returned 1.2 billion dollars to the government of Nigeria. Nigeria and Switzerland in 2016 signed a letter of intent for the repatriation of illicit assets, including the 321 million dollars allegedly stashed in Swiss banks by late Gen Sani Abacha. [34] General Abacha imprisoned former president Obasanjo on a trumped charge of planning a coup. None of the former heads of state, Ibrahim Babangida, Buhari voiced any objection in public of Obasanjo's innocence. This is because they were all afraid of their lives and the security of their families, except General T. Y. Danjuma and Joe Garba, although they made no public statement to Obasanjo's innocence but wept upon seeing their former boss languishing in jail.

Al Mustapha, the former Chief of Security for Gen Abacha, said Power in Nigeria is like a poison covered with honey and corrupt Nigerians are like flies who continue to perch on the layers of honey until they meet the fatal poison. When they decide to steal, they steal heavy so that even when they are caught, they will decide to deduct a little fraction out of it and they still remain billionaires. That is the game[35]

The bigger question is what happened to the rest of the uncollected money or what did the Nigerian government do with the recovered money?

The military regimes ruled the nation for about thirty-five years following Nigeria's independence. The General officers ruled by decree, without regards for democratic dispensation that could have provided checks and balances. The application of discretion and arbitrariness in the manner decisions were taken were without accountability. This provided avenue for corruption.

The federal, state and local governments failure to apply standards and clear operational procedure has allows officials to operate with-out discretion in the performance of duty with an eye towards corrupt practices and self-enrichment. The greatest injustice the military posed was not only the economic and financial mismanagement but the vicious cycle of military successfully replacing it-self and democracy suffers.[36]

The weak legal and judicial processes have given rise to miscarriage of justice or delay in equitable dispensation of justice. Such judicial maleficence is the case of one John Yakubu a former Assistant Director of the Police Pension Office, who allegedly stole 32 billion naira of Police pension. Upon prosecution, he claimed that the prosecuting attorney lied, that he only stole 20 billion naira. Mr. Yakubu was found guilty and sentenced to two years in jail. But the kicker was Mr. Yakubu was given an option to pay a fine of 750,000 naira. The question Mr. Yakubu and the likes of him failed to answer is how many Nigerians have died never receiving their pension or collapsed in line waiting to apply for these meager pensions after so many credible years of service to the nation of Nigeria. This was a complete mockery of Nigerian Judicial system.[37] This is compounded by blanket Immunity granted to public office holders from prosecution while in office. An example of this is Senator Buruji who is awaiting extradition to USA for drug offenses.

Weak and corrupt law enforcement apparatus in Nigeria often arise from inadequate capacity to investigate and prosecute cases. Leadership that is corrupt or perceived to be so often encourages the followership that is corrupt and follow corrupt practices. There is the absence of internal administrative controls in many government establishments to prevent fraud.

Extremely poor welfare and working conditions, which do not allow for decent living, often encourages officials to pilfer and profit form bribes. The removal of subsidies on many services provided by government and subjecting pricing of virtually every service to market forces often leaves the low and medium income group poorer thereby making them susceptible to corrupt tendencies. These are some of the factors that fuel corruption in Nigeria and the continent of Africa in general.

The increasing and widespread loss of jobs and the attendant social insecurity have challenged the perception of public servants. This is worsened by the attitude of government towards regular payment or lack of payment salaries, retirement benefits and pension of both serving and retired government employees and some state public servants. In Imo State, Nigeria, Mr. Rochas Okorocha, the State governor unilaterally slashed the salaries of state employees in 2016 and told the employees to go work in their farms. Under what authority does the state governor have to cut the salaries of state employees with-out the approval of the legislators? What is he intending to do with such revenue? In other states across the nation, those fortunate to be paid have had their salaries reduced. Widespread and pervasive poverty provokes social pressure on the few office holders. This remains a major motivation for corruption in Nigeria.

It is not uncommon to see traditional rulers award chieftaincy titles to people whose sources of wealth are questionable and whose characters are equally in disrepute. The characters of the traditional rulers themselves are dubious. It is nearly impossible to have a fox guard the chicken coop or an armed robber guard the bank but such is the character of Nigerian and African leaders. The acceptance of high societal greed is driving many Nigerians to ambiguous venture. This leaves the masses with nowhere to turn for help. Low risk coupled with the high proceeds of corruption remains a motivating factor for more corruption because no one or very few crooks are ever prosecuted. The belief that one can always "settle" that is bribe any other person that is expected to check, prevent or punish corrupt practices makes the practice less risky and the crimes advantageous and the citizens see it and condone or try to participate in these unsavory practices. Excessive materialism, weak ethical environment, erosion of moral values and lust for power and recognition are some of the other factors that fuel corruption in Nigeria. This is not independent to Nigeria; it can be translated to any African country, irrespective of size and mineral wealth.

Furthermore, members of the public are inadequately educated on its rights as well as penalties and consequences of corrupt practices. They know it is wrong but uneducated on the recourse as citizen. Or they are just afraid for dear life. Pressures exerted by transnational companies, highly placed wealthy Nigerians and high-level government officials for quick access to leadership, resources and contracts remains a major driver of corruption in Nigeria.

The down ward trend in socio-economic deterioration in Nigeria cannot be divorced from the endemic corruption which has eaten deep into the fabrics of the national life. Alison-Mudueke the nation's first and only female oil minister was arrested by Britain's National Crime Agency (NCA) and has since been charged with money laundering and bribery. The former oil minister may be facing extradition proceedings back to Nigeria. With the arrest came the seizure of 27 thousand pounds British Sterling at her home in London. EFCC the premier watch dog for financial crimes in Nigeria recently disclosed that they are on the verge of confiscating over -billion-naira worth of properties belonging to Mrs. Madueke.

President Muhammadu Buhari has revealed that some former government officials have started returning to the Federal Government's coffers, part of the public funds they looted illegally. The decision to return the money by the officials was not so voluntary or of their newly found religion, knowing that the long arm of the law will soon seize them. The amount and those who looted the public coffers during President Jonathan's regime and previous should be publicized to be publicly shamed, and this is also a deterrent. If some of these public office holders are voluntarily returning some money, how much more are they not returning? These scoundrels are still walking and breathing free air on God's green earth as free Nigerians.

The diversion of public resources in this form and inflated contracts means that fewer projects will be executed with government allocated fund. This implies that contracts awarded would either result in sub-standard job or non-completion of such contracts as is witnessed all over the country. Loss of revenue to government as a result of corrupt practices of some officials in National Port Authority and Customs, Immigration and Tax departments also indicate that not as many resources can be invested by government to complete public projects such as crumbling infrastructures, schools, hospitals, roads and bridges. Unfortunately, the proceeds of corrupt practices are not usually invested back into the community to provide employment; instead, such ill acquired wealth are spent on luxurious items of consumption, houses, cars or transfer of such funds into foreign account. With this money out of circulation, the government runs the difficulty of attracting foreign investment which decreases wealth distribution and government transparency.

The World Bank has identified power, corruption and access to finance as the bane of the private sector in Nigeria. According to the bank, this has resulted in a seventeen to twenty percent loss in sales by Nigerian firms. To make matters worse, rather than improving, electric generation, it continues dropped.

Nigeria's inability to generate and distribute enough energy is largely associated with the level of corruption in power supply sector. It has been estimated that the allocation to the Power Holding Company of Nigeria between 2001 and 2007 stood at about $10.0 billion. In spite of this, power supply in Nigeria is at best sporadic and has declined from about 3,200 to barely 2,600 mega- watts during the period. Even when the supply was temporarily disconnected as a result of faults arising from malfunctioning equipment, officials of Power Holding Company of Nigeria (PHCN) would demand bribe before repairs could be affected and service restored. This limits economic growth, resulting in high cost of production and Nigeria's export rendered uncompetitive in the global market.[38]

Gas flaring, pollution of water, farm land and air by the Oil companies are issues that are dangerous to human lives and destroy the environment in the Niger Delta region, south of Nigeria. Below is an account of misappropriation of funds as recounted by Vanguard, one of Nigeria's leading daily Newspapers entitled **Corruption: Niger Delta Development Commission (NDDC) Spends N1.3 Billion on Christmas Parties.** In pursuit of his anti-graft crusade, President Muhammadu Buhari may have to beam his searchlight on the activities of the Niger Delta Development Commission, NDDC. If the findings and documents obtained by Vanguard are anything to go by, the NDDC is a cesspool of corruption.

The documents indicated that the agency, which is being supervised by the Presidency through the Office of the Secretary to the Government of the Federation, has brazenly ignored the provisions of the Public Procurement Act, PPA, in the award of contracts for projects and services, thereby allowing its cronies to smile home with huge amounts of public funds.

The 2007 PPA sets limits on contracts that key officials of the commission can award; what the board can approve; what should be sent to the Bureau of Public Procurement, BPP, and what the Federal Executive Council should handle, in the spirit of transparency and accountability.

Under the PPA, the Managing Director of the NDDC, can award contracts that are not above N200 million while the board can approve jobs that are not above N1 billion. Specifically, any job above N1 billion must be subjected to a competitive bidding process and awarded by the FEC after being processed by the BPP, another agency under the Presidency.

However, findings show that the NDDC management had chosen to use contract-splitting as a defense to award huge contracts beyond its limit without passing through the BPP, thereby making it possible for insiders and their associates, particularly influential political elements, to make away with billions of Naira from the commission.

The commission appeared to have ignored former President Goodluck Jonathan's directive not to award new contracts but to strive to complete abandoned ones so as to clear the backlog of funds being owed local contractors.

Contrary to the Presidential directive, the new board embarked on contract bazaar within the first two weeks of its inauguration actively acquiring even second-hand exotic vehicles at the cost of new ones.

Documents at the disposal of Vanguard show that within its first two weeks the managing director single-handedly issued a local purchasing order, LPO, valued at N888, 175,500 million to a Port Harcourt-based car dealer to supply forty assorted vehicles.

Of the vehicles ordered, four were armored Sport Utility Lexus and Landcruiser vehicles valued at N213.8 million. It is not clear when the vehicles were supplied and who is using them.

Shortly after the acquisition of the expensive vehicles, the commission ordered the procurement of security vehicles for the Nigeria Police at the cost of N12.5 billion to enable the police to provide adequate security for the nine Niger Delta states of Abia, Imo, Akwa Ibom, Cross River, Bayelsa, Rivers, Edo, Delta, Edo and Ondo.

However, to prevent the huge contract from getting to the BPP and the FEC for scrutiny and approval, the commission carefully split the supply job into twelve slots and awarded it at the cost of N985 million to each of the contractors.

Not done, the NDDC shortly after awarded another contract worth N2.7b to thirty limited liability companies suspected to be owned by close associates of key officials for what it called "Intelligence-gathering and management." Each of the thirty firms got N99.7 million from the NDDC for the job which should have been handled by the security agencies.

The contract bazaar was quickly followed by another award of N1.6-billion job carefully split among eighty-five companies for the 'procurement, transportation and delivery' of waste disposal trucks to the commission.

The contract bazaar has even led to some disagreement between the board and some accounting/procurement officials. In one very despicable case, the commission ignored the professional audit query/advice not to award a 'Quick-impact' job valued at N715 million to one person to act as both contractor and consultant.

But trouble is currently brewing in the commission following the resolve of some aggrieved management staff and top officials to expose the rot in the establishment, leading to the release of financial malfeasance that has been going on in the place since the last board was inaugurated in November 2013.

One of the documents indicate that the sum of N1.3 billion was approved and released for NDDC Christian Fellowship and NDDC Children and Disable families end-of-the-year parties.

While the Christian Fellowship reportedly received N500 million, the NDDC children and disable families got N800 million.

The commission is also said to have inexplicably moved the sum of N100 billion from its Access Bank account on Agip Road branch to an undisclosed location, in the heat of the last election, in which Buhari won thereby raising eyebrow among staff and stakeholders."[39]

Conversely, because of bribes, the regulations are either unenforced or officials are influenced to ensure that penalties of such contraventions are generally too mild as to prevent more breaches or clean-up of the environmental disaster created by the Shell Oil company, British Petroleum, Exxon-Mobile and Chevron Oil company.[40]

Corrupt governance has given chance to suppressive supervision and total disregard for the rule of law making the electoral process a win at all cost. This has led to incidence of politically motivated assassinations and kidnap or imprisonment of political opponents or prominent citizens across Nigeria. For example, Bola Ige the former Attorney General of the Federation, MKO Abiola, General Musa Shehu Yar'adua, both died while imprisoned. Olusegun Obasanjo was saved by divine providence. As he recounted on *My Watch*, an angel of death was sent by the Abacha admiration visited him on two occasions but Obasanjo refused to have his blood drawn by this doctor. This was his saving grace. Obasanjo was indeed a lucky man.

Neither the state nor the federal government has done enough to address the problem of these corruptions or punish those responsible.

One local government in Rivers State dedicated only 2.4 percent of its revenues to maintaining its crumbling primary school infrastructure while spending 30 percent of its budget on salaries and expenses for the offices of its chairman and legislative councilors. Some local government chairmen have set aside more money for their own travel and "miscellaneous expenses" than they allocate to the schools and health clinics they are charged to maintain.[41]

A survey on the level of corruption in Nigeria carried out in 2003 by the Institute of Development Research of the Ahmadu Bello University, Zaria, ranked political parties in the country, third in the list of thirty most corrupt public institutions in Nigeria. This is a sad development for Nigeria because political parties are the ideological powerhouse of civilian administration. Political Parties in Nigeria have been the main avenues for promoting corrupt practices in the country through **godfatherism.** These are powerful political bosses, king makers sitting atop vast sponsorship networks that view the government, local, state and federal elections primarily through the lens of their own personal enrichment by extortion.[42] If you, as the chosen candidate, are unable to make the payment the god fathers demanded, there are other actors in line, disposed to double the godfather's payment because the reward is worth it. In the event you did not make such payment while in office, it is almost guaranteed that you will not win a re-election not only that you may even lose your life. This is not politics but indentured servitude Nigerian style. This is government by the people for the people Nigerian way. The prediction of the election results is known before the last ballot is cast and counted. This is the functional power of the godfathers.

At the 2003 Special Convention of the ruling People Democratic Party (PDP), where the presidential flag bearer was chosen, it was alleged that more than N1billon bribe was allegedly disbursed to delegates by the former President Obasanjo's group on the ninth floor of the Nicon Hilton Hotel, Abuja.[43] President Obasanjo claims that he had nothing to do with the third term bid but he did nothing to discourage it. Needless to say that a corrupt ruling party undoubtedly would always produce a corrupt government; such as the government of Musa Yar'Adua and his successor, Goodluck Jonathan before his death. Obasanjo said in *My Watch: Now and Then*, "if what is called corruption is stealing under the watch of president Jonathan, then government has become legalized and protected armed robbery"[44] The state and local governments took their cues from the corruption in Federal Capital Territory, Abuja. All entities have lost the moral courage to police the blatant corruption in which they are immersed.

It is worthy to note that the Halliburton-KBR case is not alone in the recurring tally of scandals involving multinationals cooperation and corporate corruption in Nigeria. German industrial conglomerate Siemens recently agreed to pay a $1.6 billion settlement to U.S. and European authorities for bribery of officials around the world, including Nigeria, and German courts have convicted company officials of criminal offenses for their roles in the misdeeds Schmiergeld, or "grease money." Another top executive at Willbros Inc., an oil services company, pled guilty to criminal corruption offenses under the FCPA, and the company consented to pay $32 million in penalties and disgorgement of profit for involvement in the bribery of Nigerian government officials for pipeline contracts in the country, as well as additional contracts outside of Nigeria.[45]. The executive arm of government response was the Attorney-General and Minister of Justice, Michael Aondoakaa, who threatened to sue Halliburton and its TSKJ partners both in their home countries and in the global financial centers where they do business, for $10 billion in damages. Is it not the same high government officials in his administration that accepted the bribes in the first place? How comfortable would it be for the Attorney-General and Minister of Justice, Michael Aondoakaa to prosecute his acquaintances and his boss's friends for crime against self-enrichment. In the end, no one went to jail for these crimes in Nigeria. Is it not ironic that a foreign country prosecuted and got penalties for the alleged crime while the country in which the crimes were committed paid lip service to the crime and the company?

Recently, the former President of Nigeria General Olusegun Obasanjo who has become a moral crusader of sort is not naive. He tolerated corruption during his administration. He made some significant gains against corruption but not enough. Obasanjo was fully in-charge of the petroleum ministry, where high-level corrupt practices took place with impunity. The $400 million invested on the Turn-Around Maintenance (TAM) of the oil refineries and repairs of the refineries failed to yield any positive result, and the contractors awarded the contracts were never investigated or charged for fraud.[46] Nigeria's former president, Olusegun Obasanjo, confirmed that the country's indebtedness to the London Club as at November 2006 was N270 billion (Daniel, 2006), so, the amount of misappropriated funds is more than the totality of Nigeria's indebtedness.[47] While the US Federal Bureau of Intelligence (FBI) is close to concluding an investigation of the corruption scandal, which is alleged to have reached the highest levels of the administration of former President Olusegun Obasanjo, information already in the public domain reveals that Tesler's Gibraltar-based firm, Tri Star, paid TSKJ bribes to Nigerian government officials in several installments: $40 million in 1994, $60 million in 1995, $37.5 million in 1999, $21 million in 2001 and $23 million in 2002. From these amounts, there have also been revelations about the recipients of some of the payments: $40 million to Gen. Sani Abacha in November 1994; $2.5 million into Swiss bank accounts held by a Petroleum Minister for Gen. Abacha under a false name, between 1996 and 1998; $75,000 (in two installments) to a former Inspector General of Police; $2.4 million to officials of Nigeria's Federal Inland Revenue Service (FIRS) in 2001 and 2002 to obtain favorable tax treatment; millions to officials of Nigeria National Petroleum Company (NNPC) in August 2002; $500,000 worth of Nigerian Naira to an official of NNPC; excess of $1.8 million for visas between approximately 1997 and 2004.[48]

The national company charged with safeguarding and accounting for the oil funds is the major source of the corruption. According to Obgeidi, records have shown that the Nigerian National Petroleum Corporation (NNPC) is at the center of major corrupt practices in the industry with regards to the operation of its finances, especially in respect of actual revenue realized from the sale of crude oil, and other petroleum resources, such as natural gas. It is also the NNPC that finance some of the corrupt behavior by Nigerian Leadership. Furthermore Revenue Mobilization Allocation and Fiscal Commission (RMAFC) indicated that 445,000 barrels of crude oil sold by the NNPC between January and July 2002 was not accounted for in its financial report. The report further indicated that within the seven-month period, there was a windfall of N302 billion as undeclared revenue. The request by Haman Tukur, Chairman of RMAFC, to the Presidency to compel Jackson Gaius-Obaseki, former Group Managing Director of NNPC, to refund the remaining money into government's coffer was never heeded. More so, the joint panel of the National Assembly set up to probe the matter was also hindered by the Presidency and top hierarchy officials of the People Democratic Party on the ground that the probe would send negative signals abroad about corruption in Nigeria, particularly because the Presidency directly oversees the petroleum ministry.[49] Similar probe got the former Governor of Central bank of Nigeria, Sanusi, dismissed from his post by President Goodluck Jonathan. Vincent Azie, acting Auditor-General of the Federation, showed that the amount represented financial frauds ranging from embezzlement, payments for jobs not done, double-debiting, inflation of contract figures to release of money without the consent of the approving authority in ten major ministries.

Rather than cautioning the ministers whose ministries were named in the fraud or invite the Independent Corrupt Practices Commission (ICPC) to further investigate the veracity of the alleged fraud, Vincent Azie was hastily retired by the Presidency for procedural offences.[50]

Foreign companies have become very savvy in the Nigeria's corrupt business practices that a questionable French company won the contract at the cost of 214 million dollars to produce the Nigerian Identity Cards, such as the social security card in USA or the national identity card of Great Britain under the leadership of President Obasanjo. It was alleged that seven prominent public servants collaborated with SAGEM S.A. to scuttle the $214 million project. Records of the investigation into the matter indicted Hussaini Akwanga (who, until December 4, 2003, was Nigeria's Minister for Labor and Productivity) Chief Sunday Michael Afolabi and Mahmud Shata (former Minister of Internal Affairs and Minister of State in the same Ministry respectively), R. O. Akerele Permanent Secretary of the same Ministry of Internal Affairs, Okwesilieze Nwodo (former Governor of Enugu State and erstwhile secretary of the ruling People Democratic Party), Niyi Adelagun (a business partner of SAGEM S.A. in Nigeria), and Jean-Pierre Delarue (the Regional Area Manager, Identification Systems of SAGEM S.A). It is now on the pages of history books that the huge sum released for the project that was not fully executed and the fund was divided among the suspected culprits.[51]

People should make " hay" while the sun shines is not struggling to provide for your family in time of plenty for leaner times but a synonym for corruption. That means steal as much as you can because you may never get that opportunity again. To put this level of corruption into perspective, it is estimated that since independence which was October 1, 1960 to 1999, past Nigerian leaders had stolen or misused $407 billion or 225 billion pounds. This amount is equal to all western aid given to the continent of Africa during this same period. Yet they have the audacity to ask for more debt relief.[52] The poverty level in the Niger Delta, in spite of their oil keeps growing. The youths are aggrieved and radicalized by the activities of government and oil firms into the Movement for the Survival of the Ogoni People (MOSOP), in the Abacha years, and intensified with the "murder" of Ken Saro-Wiwa and eight other Ogoni activists. The people demanded an equitable share of the proceeds of oil revenues to improve their living the lives of their children and environmental conditions.[53] This was simply the reason for the murder of Saro-Wiwa and the Ogoni eight activists.

While Nigeria's federal government has made some efforts to combat corruption and improve the transparency of its finances, it has failed to address rampant corruption at the federal, state and local levels. Anti-corruption efforts have been hobbled by the government's failure to reform a political system that often rewards politicians who use corruption and violence to subvert the democratic process, especially at the state and local levels.[54] Abdulmumin Jibrin, former House chairman of Appropriation, has revealed that the House of Representatives of which he is a member is corrupt. Jibrin, when asked if former President Olusegun Obasanjo was right in saying the National Assembly was corrupt, said: "Yes, we're corrupt."

Jubrin had accused Speaker Yakubu Dogara, his deputy, Yusuf Lasun, House Whip, Alhassan Doguwa, and Minority Leader, Leo Ogor, of padding the 2016 Appropriation Bill with up to N40 billion.[55]

Leadership by example is a major requirement for a successful war against corruption. Obasanjo was a good follower before he became a good leader. If many Nigerian leaders had his consideration, Nigeria would have been a different place than the present presentation of Nigeria. The fight against corruption will necessarily have to start from the highest levels of the government. Leaders should act what they preach. A situation whereby leaders speak against corruption, and in reality, every event surrounding such leaders clearly shows proof of corruption. This will not help the struggle. African leaders should make a personal commitment to live up to the obligations of forgoing an unethical destiny for their nation.[56]

Besieged by a multitude of hostile forces, most of the leaders in Nigeria and Africa are politically insecure. They are so completely engrossed in the struggle for survival that they are hardly able to address the problem of development, crime and insecurity.[57] The illegal activities such as the advance fee fraud (known as 419) may not have been invented by Nigerians, but it is now being practiced all over the continent of Africa and beyond. Money laundering has torn the fabric of African society. Corruption, when not controlled, is far more dangerous than drug trafficking or other crimes because, the public loses confidence in the legal system and those who enforce the law.[58] This is the single most complex dilemma facing Nigeria and the continent of Africa.

The Department of State Services (DSS), equivalent to Federal Bureau of Investigation (FBI) in USA said it invaded the houses of the immediate past National Security Adviser, Mohammed Sambo Dasuki, based on 'credible intelligence linking him with "alleged plans to commit treasonable felony against the Nigerian state". Items found in his residence include seven high assault weapons, several magazines and military related gears. The team also recovered twelve (12) new vehicles, out of which five were bullet proof. SAMBO retired from the Army as a Colonel, was a former National Security Adviser to President Jonathan. Even as NSA, such guards should have been withdrawn after his dismissal, since he would not have been entitled to such armed guards. [59] This is further evidence of the diversion of public resources to protect or consolidate ill acquired personal gain. To compound his problems, Dasuki has also been charged with misappropriation of over 2 billion dollars in arm procurement by the current administration of President Buhari. To futher demonstrate the banality of the Jonathan's administration, former Finance Minister Mrs. Nenadi Usman has shed light on how she shared N23 billion among Northeast states at the insistance of former Petroleum Resources Minister Mrs. Diezani Alison-Madueke for the prosecution of last year's presidential election which Jonathan lost. Nigerians are lucky that Goodluck Jonathan did not win; had he won the 2015 election the Nigerian Government, the PDP ruling party and it leaders would have been a den of thieves.

President Obasanjo's indictment of Goodluck Jonathan, the past president of Nigeria is unequivocal. President Johnathan's administration may be the worse in terms of corruption seen in Nigeria since the second republic. Scholars are still evaluating Jonathan and his cronies, including Ngozi Okonjo Iwuala the one time World Bank Economist. Soon the chicken will come home to roost.

African leaders must realize that Public office is public trust and betrayal of that trust in any way makes the public office holder a traitor.[60] According to Obasanjo, " if in the past, corruption was in the corridors of power it would seem now that it is in the living room and bed room of power" and the bed room of power in this case is the presidency of every country on the African continent. What does this say about Nigeria and its citizens? Once Nigeria was considered the anchor and a bellwether of economic activities on the African continent, blessed by clever and energetic people and favored with an ample oil resource but despite the size and wealth. Nigeria lingers in the doldrums, constantly threatened with disintegration, economically plundered and mismanaged by her leaders. By Judge Ajibola's account, corruption has been democratized in Nigeria and the nation is experiencing corruption in absolute terms, a glaring deficit in enviable national character and general moral rectitude.[61]

Prof. Osibanjo, the Vice President of Nigeria said Corruption is an existential threat to Nigeria both as a nation and as a viable economic entity. Clearly, there is no doubt whatever whether every arm of the government can exist. The truth of the matter is that we all know that corruption is systemic in Nigeria. Every arm of the government is involved in this systemic and life threatening social anomaly called corruption. This is the first time an elected official acknowledge that corruption is depriving Nigeria of achieving its full potential.

President Jonathan, in an interview with CNN, denied that there was corruption in his administration. He is either in denial, has no clue what is happening in Nigeria, or is the chief architect of corruption, hence the denial, he is living under a rock, the ASO ROCK , somewhere outside Nigeria or he is hallucinating.

All of this is true of Jonathan or a combination thereof, you make the choice. It is well known that the Ijaw nation brews very strong kinkana, ogogoro, kpeteshi maybe, he imbibes in it that he is in so much denial on the affairs of Nigeria. Corruption has weakened Nigeria so much that she is not being seriously considered in the international community.

From L-R (1960-2015) President Nnamdi Azikiwe, Sir Abubaka Tafawa Balewa, Obafemi Awolowo, Gen. JTU Aguiyi Ironsi, Gen. Yakubu Gowan, Gen. Murtala Mohammed, Gen. Olusegun Obasanjo, President Shehu Shagari, Umaru Dikko, Gen. Buhari, Gen. Ibrahim Babangida, Gen. Sani Abacha Goodluck Jonathan

TOGO became independent on April. 27, 1960 like most African countries. The regime of Nicolas Grunitzky was on Jan. 13, 1967 toppled in a bloodless army coup led by Lt. Col. Gnanssingbé Eyadèma. Eyadèma served in the French army (1953–61) before entering the armed forces of Togo, where he became (1965) Chief of the General Staff. He seized power in 1967 and assumed the offices of president and minister of National Defense. It must be said that Grunitzky replaced his cousin Sylvanus Olympio after his assassination. After an interlude of government by military council, Eyadèma was confirmed overwhelmingly as president in elections in 1972. He proved intolerant of growing opposition, repressing dissent in trade unions and other areas of public life and activism. Government efforts to exert increased control over the economy in the late 1970s included land-reform projects and state supervision of the textile trade. A new constitution was approved in 1979, which ended emergency military rule, proclaimed the Third Togolese Republic, and renewed Togo's status as a single-party state. Eyadèma was also elected to another term as president. In 1993, Eyadèma won reelection in a contest that was boycotted by the main opposition parties. As a result, economic sanctions were imposed by the European Union. He won again in 1998, and in 1999, his party swept parliamentary elections; once again. The elections again, were boycotted by the opposition. In 2002, the constitution was amended to permit the president to seek a third term, and in the presidential election in 2003 Eyadèma was returned to office. Is there any credibility that one man can rule a nation and won over whelming majority after thirty years in office? After all the government of North Korea wins overwhelmingly without opposition. The opposition accused the government of electoral fraud. Gilchrist Olympio, The most popular opposition leader living in exile and barred from contesting. He survived a bloody ambush on his motorcade, escaped from a coup that saw his father – Togo's first post-independence leader – gunned down at the door of the American embassy, and then he later managed to avoid two death sentences pronounced by the country's courts.[62] Now, as the perpetual leader of tiny Togo's political opposition, Eyadèma died in Feb. 2005. The army engineered the appointment of Faure Essozimna Gnassingbé, Eyadèma's son, to the presidency, contrary to the constitution, which called for the speaker of parliament to succeed in the event of the president's death in the office. Parliament subsequently approved the move and amended the constitution to avoid a new election. These moves were protested internationally and sparked confrontations between Togolese demonstrators and police; Togo also was threatened with the loss of foreign aid. Under pressure Gnassingbé agreed to step down.[63]

Although Togo has government organizations that investigate corruption, it is a common business practice and remains a problem for businesses. Despite corruption being common, the government is taking steps to reduce corruption. In 2011, the government effectively implemented procurement reforms to increase transparency, with the hope of reducing corruption. New government procurements are now announced in a weekly government publication. Once contracts are awarded, all bids and the winner are published in the weekly government procurement publication.

Like many African countries, providing a gift (including cash, land, and livestock) is a common business practice. Providing gratuity is reported to result in files, documents, permits, or licenses being processed quickly resulting in a competitive and comparative advantage for companies willing or able to engage in corrupt activities. This is according to the Central Intelligence Agency of the US.

The police, gendarmes, courts and an anti-corruption committee are charged with combating corruption in Togo and remain the source of the corruption. A few Togolese officials have been prosecuted and convicted of corruption-related charges, but these cases are relatively rare and appear to involve mostly those who have in some way lost official favor.[64]

L-R Nicholas Grunitzky, Sylvanus Olympio with JFK, Gnanssingbé Eyadèma, Faure Gnassingbé

Liberia was founded in 1821, when officials of the American Colonization Society were granted possession of Cape Mesurado by local De chiefs for the settlement of freed American slaves. African-American immigrants landed in 1822, the first of some 15,000 to settle in Liberia. In 1980, William Tolbert, the president of Liberia, who had been in power for over thirty years, was assassinated in a coup led by Master Sergeant Samuel K. Doe. Pledging a return to civilian rule in 1981, the Doe government unleashed a campaign to subdue and brutalize opposition. In 1984, the military government instituted a series of constitutional reforms that included shortening the presidential term and outlawing the formation of a one-party state. Doe became Liberia's first indigenous president by fraudulent election in 1985. The Doe government was wicked for corruption and human-rights abuses; he also became the target of numerous coup attempts. During this period, thousands of refugees fled to Guinea and Côte d'Ivoire.

The April 1980 coup d'état marked the beginning of **Liberia**'s steep descent into crisis. In 1981, trans-national trade declined by approximately 67.8 percent; domestic production declined and the problems in balance of payments set in. On the fiscal side, revenue earnings decreased by approximately eight percent as a result of reduced income from taxes. This was a direct consequence of low productivity and unemployment. A decade of poor governance from 1980 to 1990, mismanagement and dictatorship led to the outbreak of civil war in late 1989 and fourteen consecutive years of bedlam, plunder, and violence which did not end until the arrival of international peacekeepers, the ousting of the Taylor Government, and signing of the Accra Comprehensive Peace Agreement (CPA) in 2003.

Late in 1989, Liberia was invaded from Côte d'Ivoire by rebel forces of the National Patriotic Front of Liberia (NPFL), led by Charles Taylor, who proclaimed himself president after Samuel Doe's assassination in 1990.

It must be said that Charles Taylor, a former warlord and friend of former Libyan strong man Muammar Qaddafi, financed the war using the illegal diamond trade and with help from employing child Soldiers. This instituted a dastard practice called shot sleeve, violent amputation of the hand at the elbow and long sleeve and such amputation at the wrist is named long sleeve.

The damage and negative consequences of the conflict were enormous. Commercial and industrial activities ceased as various warlords vied to control the country and its mineral resources. Families were shattered; entire communities were uprooted; and social, political, economic, and traditional governance systems were destroyed. There was a massive exodus of skilled and talented individuals from the country. The economy completely collapsed. GDP fell a catastrophic ninety percent between 1987 and 1995, one of the largest economic collapses ever recorded in the world similar to the economic collapse of Zimbabwe, according to the World Bank's World Development Indicators. Corruption—in the sense of bribes, payoffs and kickbacks—is only one type of government failure. Rule of law, a key governance indicator, was non-existent, further exacerbating the situation Liberia became a free for all. In Liberia, during the period, there was no investment in human capital, in infrastructure, and the environment was neglected—powerful elites took the money that could have been spent on these programs.

In 2003, United States sent troops to the area when the NPFL threatened to take foreign hostages.

Indications of what happened during the transitional period between Charles Taylor's departure and the inauguration of the Johnson-Sirleaf, a Harvard trained economist. The first woman to be elected head of state of an African country. Johnson Sirleaf served as assistant minister of finance (1972–73) under President William Tolbert and as finance minister (1980–85) in Samuel K. Doe's military dictatorship. She became known for her personal financial integrity which clashed with both Heads of State. During Doe's regime, she was imprisoned twice and narrowly avoided execution. In the 1985 national election, she campaigned for a seat in the Senate and openly criticized the military government, which led to her arrest and a ten-year prison sentence.[65]

Liberians enthusiastically went to the polls in what seemingly appeared to have been, an expression of a general desire to look up to one overarching authority vested in Mr. Charles Ghangay Taylor to rule with mandates unsurpassed by previous authorities on the Liberian Political scene. Charles Taylor wasted no time in invalidating the notion that he would transform himself into a respectable Liberian Statesman. Instead, he adopted a more aggressive posture toward the oppositions in Liberia and at times, directing his agents to murder opponents; as in the case of the Dokies and six followers of Taylor's arch-rival, Roosevelt Johnson. It is estimated that Taylor's ill- acquired wealth, is reported to be close to the tune of $450 million, such corruption created stampede amongst Taylor's officials to get rich fast while their fellow Liberians scrap for their daily necessities of life. This bubbling disorder and maneuvering for wealth and power amplified the danger of unrest assiduous over Liberia. Amid this unremarkable new wealth of Taylor and his officials, Taylor appears oblivious to the level of mass suffering and starvation induced by uncontrolled corruption of scarce public resources.[66] According to a recent Memorandum written by Liberia's Deputy Minister of National Security, Mr. John B. Wonpoe Yormie, a copy of which was obtained by the Perspective, Taylor's friend and Minister of Lands, Mines & Energy, Jenkins Dunbar, was alleged by the Memorandum of " knowingly aided and abetted the perpetration of defrauding the Government of Liberia [$354,653.00 US] in custom revenues." Jenkins Dunbar along with some close colleagues of Taylor's such as Emmanuel Shaw, Cyril Allen, Grace Minor, Robert Bright and Dan Chea are reportedly in collusion with alleged suspected international criminal individuals seemingly involved in shady business deals. Niko Shefer and Felix Kramer, two South African businessmen with questionable business history brought into the country by Shaw and Dunbar under the guise of the Greater Ministries International a "religious and charitable organization". Initially, the Greater Ministries International went to Liberia supposedly to participate in the provision of relief services for Liberians affected by the country's civil war. The Greater Ministries International, in concert with high-powered friends like Shaw and Dunbar, secured custom and tax import exemptions reserved only for relief and charitable organizations to import "donated equipment and supplies " for mineral exploration in Lower Lofa and Sinje in Cape Mount County; two places that form the heart of Liberia's Diamond Country. No longer hiding its fraudulent motive, the Director of the Board of Greater Ministries International Rev. James W. List of Tampa, Florida, on May 6, 1998 asked his friend Minister Dunbar to intervene on their behalf. The Greater Ministries International later changed its name to the Greater Diamond Company, Ltd. though the purported company pocketed over half a million dollars in duty free imports exemptions reportedly at the request of Minister Dunbar. Niko Shefer and Felix Kramer were the founders of the failed and fraudulent Amalia Gold & Diamond Group Venture that included Shefer's Tanden Group of Companies of South Africa and as well as the Greater Ministries International. With the money from the diamond mine, Taylor aided rebels in Sierra Leone during the brutal civil war in the 1990s which left 50,000 people dead and many more wounded and disfigured.

Thousands more were left mutilated in the conflict that became known for the extreme cruelty of rival rebel groups who hacked off the limbs of their victims and carved their initials into opponents.

Taylor helped to plan attacks in return for "blood diamonds" mined by slave laborers in Sierra Leone and political influence in the volatile West African region. He ensures maximum hold on the logging industry by having stakes in every logging company operating in Liberia. The most important of these companies is the Oriental Timber Company (OTC), which has President Charles Taylor as 50% stakeholder.[67]

Under international pressure, Sirleaf Johnson requested in March 2006, that Nigeria, the country Mr. Taylor fled to when his position was untenable and the heat from the international community, was becoming excessive. Reluctantly, President Obasanjo extradite Charles Taylor, who was on his way to Libya through Niger Republic. He was then brought before an International Tribunal in Sierra Leone to face war crimes charges arising from events during the Sierra Leone civil war, his trial was later transferred to The Hague for security and corruption purposes; he was convicted of war crimes in 2012 and received what amounted to life in prison.[68] In March 2007, former interim president Bryant was arrested and charged with embezzling government funds while in office. The Liberian Truth and Reconciliation Commission, which had conducted a four-year investigation of the nation's civil strife, issued its report in July 2009 and recommended that the president, and many other senior politicians who originally supported Charles Taylor, be banned from politics for thirty years in the 2011 presidential election.

The crafty misguided maneuverings of the wild-eyed contingent of hustlers masqueraded as "liberators" and pretended to be patriots of Liberia bent on removing the Taylor regime. These men are skillful at manipulation and exploitations, some aligned themselves with the insurgency groups, Liberian United for Reconciliation and Democracy (LURD), Movement for Democracy in Liberia MODEL (MODEL), etc. with their sights set intensely on the public coiffeurs. It is the boundless self-absorption rather than alleviation of misfortunes that Liberians experience living under authoritarian rule was their primary motive.

Samuel Wlue, fired from his job in Philadelphia turned up as a high-ranking official of MODEL, one of the two rebel groups that battled the deposed Liberian dictator Charles Taylor for control of Liberia. He represented

MODEL at the joint ECOWAS and international community brokered peace conference in Accra, Ghana in 2003. As the result of the peace conference, MODEL, LURD and the Taylor regime carved up strategic government bureaucracies as "spoils of war." MODEL secured the Ministry of Commerce, Bureau of Maritime and Foreign Affairs Ministry, among others. Samuel Wlue was then awarded the Commerce Ministry portfolio. For full disclosure, it is important to reveal the ties between Samuel Wlue and Emmanuel Dolo. They attended graduate school together in the US at Erskine Theological Seminary in Due West, South Carolina, where both men studied the Christian Ministry. They were roommates before Samuel Wlue's transferred from Erskine to continue his studies at the Southern Baptist Theological Seminary in Raleigh, North Carolina.[69] In short, they lied to protect the interest of their friend and not look out for the interest and integrity of the Liberian State. Samuel Wlue was sending 4,000 dollars to his wife in US every month. The question not asked is how is this man capable of sending his wife such amount every month from Liberia? It is usually the other way. The likes of Senators Price Johnson, Adolphus Dolo, Isaac Nyenabo, Saah Gbolee and other human hawks who shares intimacy through political war criminal acquaintance seems to be the covert hands behind this clever hatchet bill of impunity. Nyanebo might be rewarded for contributing to the slaughtering of half a million Liberians during the fourteen-year civil war' by being re-elected to the post of Senior Senator.

Development will never come to Liberia if Liberians continue to rely on foreign companies for bailout. History attests to this. The Indian, Ghanaian, Nigerian and Lebanese business communities in Liberia have never productively participated in Liberia's development. In fact, they have always tended to set themselves apart from Liberia. It is up to the government and people of Liberia to build-up their country's credibility to attract investors to boost the Liberian economy.[70] Transparency international confirm that about half of the post war countries revert to war within one decade and corruption is considered as one of the major factors that contribute to fueling the conflict and the return to violence. Therefore, overcoming corruption in post-war Liberia is essential to restoring the confidence of Liberians at home and abroad is significant. In 2012, the Liberian central government dismissed or suspended a number of officials for corruption. Auditor General Robert L. Kilby and General Services Agency Director General Pealrine Davis-Parkinson were dismissed for conflicts of interest.

Deputy Justice Minister Freddie Taylor, Deputy Bureau of Immigration and Naturalization (BIN) Commissioner Robert Buddy, former solicitor general Micah Wright, and Border Patrol Chief Wilson Garpeh were dismissed for alleged involvement in human trafficking. [71]

Deputy Public Works Minister Victor B. Smith was suspended for allegedly violating the law but was reinstated a week later following an investigation. President Sirleaf dismissed the chairman and other board members of the Liberia Airports Authority amid corruption allegations. An assistant Labor Minister was also dismissed for issuing work permits to foreigners after allegedly taking bribe. These are all steps in the right direction but these men should have gone to jail as a disincentive for deceitful business men, politicians and ordinary citizens in Liberia.

L-R William Tolbert, Samuel Doe with Former President Reagan and the US Defense Secretary Casper Weinberger, Charles Taylor, Ellen Johnson, lady with short sleeve due to blood diamond and civil war.

Sierra Leone gained independence in 1961. The Sierra Leone under Stevens is like a time bomb waiting to explode. Stevens took power after a revolt led by low-ranking soldiers. He pushed through a new constitution outlawing all opposition to his All Peoples Congress (A.P.C.). Although he served as opposition leader during the government of his predecessor, Prime Minister Sir Albert Margai, Stevens now claims that the idea of competitive politics is alien to Sierra Leone's people. Says he: "We don't understand the concept of a loyal opposition." The governor of the central bank, Samuel

Bangura, objected to what he described as Stevens' plans to pocket a large portion of Libya's $5 million contribution toward defraying the costs of the O.A.U. summit. Bangura was found dead outside his mansion. Police at first called his death suicide.

Stevens often confuses the national bank account with his own.[72] The country is mineral rich with natural resources such as gold, diamond, bauxite. These resources have failed to yield the revenue or improve the lives of ordinary Sierra Leoneans. Government officials have been involved in the illegal transactions of these natural resources thereby defrauding the government and the people of Sierra Leone.

Foday Sankoh, the Sierra Leonean warlord, and the leader of the Revolutionary United Front (RUF) began his political career in the 1970s as a critic of widespread corruption. Sierra Leone's military and political elite were plundering the diamond and other mineral wealth of the tiny nation, whose people are considered to be among the world's poorest.

The high-minded crusade to eliminate corruption soon degenerated, as impoverished young men sought to make their own providence.

One can say that Sankoh has nine lives because he was captured but escaped detention facing a death sentence. His RUF mounted a formidable attack on Freetown which was repulsed by Nigerian Peace Keeping Force. The RUF quickly earned a savage reputation, as they amputated limbs of civilians, routinely raped women and girls and abducted boys as child Soldiers to join their army. Young recruits were often forced to rape or kill a family member, thus preventing a return to their previous lives. RUF young soldiers were often forcibly injected with cocaine before going into battle. With a mind so messed –up, they were divorced from what is considered sane and committed atrocities under altered state of mind.

Sankoh joined other Sierra Leonean dissidents in Libya, where COL. Muammar al-Gaddafi was sponsoring revolutionary movements throughout the world. He later went to Liberia, where he joined forces with another young charismatic—and ruthless revolutionary leader Charles Taylor, who became president of his country after a brutal civil war. Sankoh subsequently received amnesty in return for signing the July 1999 peace treaty.[73]

Sierra Leone is no different from the other African countries relative to corruption. The emergence of Ebola disease compounded and brought Sierra Leonean and Liberian economies to a stand-still in 2014-2015. In the absence of natural disaster and civil war, corruption is crippling the nation of Sierra

Leone. The nature of corruption in this country is in the form of bribe paid to government officials in the award of large government contracts, misappropriation of public funds and direct request for bribe from police and custom officials and workers in other ministries in the discharge of their duties. Drug trafficking and money laundering has increased such that Sierra Leone has become a trans-shipment hub for distribution of drugs heading to Europe from South America. Seven hundred kilograms of cocaine was seized at the Lungi National Airport in 2008 from an aircraft coming from Venezuela. Since its founding, the Anti- Corruption Commission (ACC) has fingered officials throughout the government for corruption. The list of cases reads like an almanac entry on Sierra Leonean government officials. On June 9, 2000, Sierra Leone's Marine Resources Minister Lawrence Kamara was accused of embezzling $45,000 US in government funds. Though he was forced to resign and write the administration a check for the missing $45,000 US, sadly, he was not prosecuted. On March 9, 2001, Sierra Leone's Agriculture Minister Dr. Harry Will was convicted of embezzling $1.5m US from World Bank development funds meant to buy rice seed from Ghana for struggling Sierra Leonean farmers. This was a similar crime committed by Nigeria's Umaru Dikko during Shahu Shagari's government. Justice Mohamed Taju Deen, who fined Dr. Will a mere Le 500,000 ($250 US), was in turn convicted of accepting bribes in exchange for the light sentence, a week after Will's conviction, a court convicted Soluku Bockarie, permanent secretary at the Ministry of Education, for misappropriating roughly $1 billion US from funds meant to pay the salaries of Sierra Leone's 26,000 teachers. Over the course of the trial, Bockarie also fingered his boss, Education Minister Dr. Alpha Wurie, but the court dismissed the testimony, claiming Bockarie was a doomed man desperate to drag everyone down with him.[74] The court refused to understand that where there is smoke, there is fire. The evidence against Wurie may not have been strong or convincing, does not mean that he is innocent. On Sept. 8, 2001, British-born Inspector General of Police Keith Biddle ordered the suspension and arrest of forty-one police officers for accepting bribes from motorists and diamond smugglers. In an effort to silence Paul Kamara, on Nov. 2, 2001 and acting on direct orders from the president, the Anti -Crime Commission began investigating editor of the leading daily newspaper, For di People, Paul Kamara for tax evasion. Kamara has been an outspoken critic of the government Sierra Leone. He was eventually cleared of the charge. The causes of political corruption in Sierra Leone range from sheer greed of the established elite to low wages of public officials such as teachers and police personnel to sociological factors. But irrespective of the cause, a common characteristic of this obnoxious activity is politicians acquiring wealth and prestige through a system of rapacious accumulation leading to the belief, "if he can do it and get away with it, why can't I?" This crimes are not primary to Sierra Leone but in every nation on the African continent. This Predatory accumulation also allows politicians in Sierra Leone to enter into profitable businesses while simultaneously allocating monopoly rights in the economy and distributing public resources according to patrimonial logic.[75] These are decisions about resources made by 'big men' and their cronies, who are linked by 'informal' private and personal, patronage and clientelist networks that exist outside before, beyond and despite the state structure, and who follow a logic of personal and particular interest rather than national betterment. [76] This illustrates how state agents can use the power they are armed with to sustain their status and wealth, thereby deviating from the moral principles of the modern state.

The systematic development of high-cost services in the education and healthcare sectors clearly advantages the minority urban elite and high-wage earners at the detriment of the majority of Sierra Leoneans who are low-wage breadwinners.[77] Sierra Leone has not provided a business-friendly environment, which explains why the country has consistently ranked lower than many African countries in the last five years on the ease of doing business. Additionally, corruption has raised the cost of doing business in Sierra Leone through the introduction of a new set of transactional costs. This includes the cost of negotiating, monitoring and enforcing illegal agreements. Thus, the composition of government expenditure is distorted as corrupt politicians are more likely to choose government expenditure not on the basis of public welfare but on the basis of the opportunity for exploitation and bribery.[78] Sierra Leone experienced a brutal civil war from 1991-2001. Entrenched corruption and mismanagement of the country's resources were the root causes of the war but greed and violence were the product of the war. Sierra Leone's application for Millennium Challenge Corporation (MCC) funding is under consideration again, after it was not put up for a vote last year because it did not pass MCC's control of corruption indicator. From 2003 to 2012, a ten-year period for which audit reports by the country's auditing department recorded that around **Le1,166,564,381,817.40 (over one TRILLION Leones)** were stolen from the country's finances. In dollar terms (using an average exchange rate of $1=Le4,000), this amounts to about **$291,540,237.54 (almost over two hundred and ninety-one MILLION dollars)**. This is close to the amount the

Sierra Leone Government will get if its MCC application is approved.

In Ghana, the use of public office for private gain has been in existence before independence. But the politics of corruption is a daily feed in Ghanaian political diet, this opinion is informed by dramatic lifestyles of public officials in the face of wide spread poverty; and Rawlings the former Revolutionary Ruling Council Chairman, armed with more emotional shrewdness than cerebral quotient, projected himself as "Mr. Spotless," and knows how to dine in the corrupt connoisseur to his advantage in the face of weak rational attention to Ghanaians corruption dilemma.[79] This mixed handsome Irish-Ghanaian extraction is a charismatic leader with a brain the size of drosophila's in an over grown skull. A well-beloved leader and state's man, one may even say charming and magnetic during his time in Ghana leadership. His command of the English language is next to the former Biafran leader, Ojukwu's. He has a command presence when he walks into a room and when he speaks. With eyes bulging like a balloon that seemed to pop out anytime and veins in his neck pulsating and spit flying from both sides of his mouth when he talks, hands gesticulating, Rawlings looks like a man possessed.

In 1979, when Ft. Lt Jerry John Rawlings (popularly known as J.J) emerged on the troubled Ghanaian political and military scene, it was to purify the country of corruption from the military to civilian regimes; Rawlings, like General Buhari of Nigeria, thought there was so much corruption that it had hindered the wheels of progress.

By all indications, much of the corruption dialogues were more mired in the long-running military regimes. The political corruption game that saw regimes overthrown goes like this: Gen Joseph Ankrah military regime overthrew the President Kwame Nkrumah administration, the first president of Ghana in 1966, while on a state visit to North Vietnam and China. President Kwame Nkrumah is the founder of Pan Africanism, a movement that intended to unit Africans and its resources against foreign exploitation. Africa and African resources for Africa. He was unceremoniously overthrown in a bloodless coup d'état. Later that same year, Seymour Hersch of the *New York Times*, citing "first hand intelligence sources," defended Stockwell's account, claiming that "many CIA operatives in Africa considered the agency's role in the overthrow of Mr. Nkrumah to have been pivotal."

The coup was actually undertaken by Generals Emmanual Kotoka and Akwesi Amankwah Afrifa, and Gen. Ankrah was picked as Head of State due to his position and date of rank. Akwesi Afrifa toppled the Gen. Ankrah regime in 1969. Gen. Kutu Acheampong overthrew Prime Minister Dr. Kofi Busia/President Edward Akuffo-Addo administration in 1972. Gen F.W.K Akuffo's military junta had overthrown the Gen. Acheampong in 1978. Flight LT John Jerry Rawlings overthrew the Gen Akuffo and Dr. Hilla Liman regimes in 1979 and 1981 respectively. This is the African way of assuming State leadership.

The overthrow of Gen Akuffo was the bloodiest, Rawlings and his Armed Forces Revolutionary Council (AFRC) publicly executing the likes of Gen Afrifa, Gen Acheampong, Gen. Kotei, among others, for alleged corrupt practices. This was probably due to the fact that the former general officers were due to execute Rawlings for an attempted coup before he was sprung from the jail by Soldiers in his Unit. The corruption issues were thought to be so serious by Rawlings and his AFRC that COL Roger Felli, a Foreign Affairs Commissioner (Minister) under Gen. Acheampong, was killed for having just $300 US in his foreign accounts.

The coup plotters view corruption, pillage, concentration of wealth in hands of a few, increasing joblessness, universal mismanagement particularly of the country's wealth, election malpractices and other types of political charade and tribalism as the main factors leading to the overthrow of the previous government. Once in power, these self-righteous indignant set out to address other agenda but the ones they proposed as the reason for the revolution. For Rawlings, none of his associates were corrupt but the rest of Ghanaians were, even if there are incontrovertible evidences to the contrary. Rawlings is always defending in a threatening manner his associates implicated in corrupt practices.

Perhaps to intimidate and threaten the judiciary, Rawlings was a familiar face in law courts where some of his associates are indicted for financial crimes. The implication is that Rawlings does not trust judiciary and sees all indictments against his associates for financial crimes as politically motivated. In this context, Rawlings actions undermine the rule of law as a mechanism to fight corruption.

For Rawlings, Tsatsu Tsikata, former head of Ghana's National Oil Company, a Rawlings appointee and family member, who has been jailed five years for financial crimes, is innocent, but other Ghanaians in a similar situation aren't. Critically, by indicting Tsikata, a very close adviser to Rawlings, it implies that Rawlings himself has been indicted for financial crimes. Not surprisingly,

Kwabena Agyepong, a former presidential spokesman for President Kufuor, has revealed that Rawlings knew and encouraged Tsikata's financial crimes. Ghanaians were shocked when a Norwegian court implicated officials from Scancem, a company that formerly owned Ghanacem, the cement producing company. Scancem officials are said to have paid millions of dollars to Rawlings' associates to ensure that they would retain the monopoly of cement production in Ghana. By maintaining the monopoly on cement, they can control the price of cement. The money allegedly went to former Rawlings' presidential advisor, PV Obeng who was effectively a defacto Prime Minister under Rawlings' military junta Provisional National Defence Council. Rawlings owes Ghanaians an explanation as to how $7 million US went missing from a total of $10 million US, secured by the government of Ghana for the refurbishment of Tema Food Processing Factory[80]. Rowlings sold Nsawam canary to Caridem . If you lifted the veil of incorporation, you will see Rowlings' wife, Nana Konadu, as the owner.

In 1981, when Chairman Rawlings came to power, Ghana's Shipping Line, the Black Star Line, had fourteen vessels. These were ships that belonged to the Republic of Ghana. By the time Rawlings left power, he had shut down the Black Star Line which Nkrumah had built, sold all of the fourteen vessels, kept the purse and rendered fellow Ghanaian citizens who worked as seamen and merchant marines jobless[81].

Corruption has been a problem in every government since Independence. Every government has come into office with a pledge to fight corruption but has been tainted by it. This is made worse. There is no law governing gifts and hospitality offered to civil servants, and facilitation payments are not defined in law. A Southwark Crown Court ruled that during the 1990's, the British Construction firm, Mabey and Johnson, paid Ghana government officials bribes, ranging from 500 pounds to 55,000 pounds in order to secure contracts worth about 26 million pounds sterling. Amongst the Ghanaian officials named are Mr. George Sipa Yankey, the Minister of Health, Mr. Kwame Peprah, the former Minister of Finance and current Chairman of Board of Directors of SSNIT, Dr Quarshie and Alhaji Siddique Boniface. While we focus on corruption amongst politicians, it is only the tip of the iceberg. As the involvement of a then civil servant in the London court case demonstrates, civil servants are very often not immune to corruption.

Indeed, while the involvement of politicians make headlines, petty corruption, involving the Police, the Judiciary and the Civil Service retards development and frustrates the public even more.[82] Low-level government employees are known to ask for a 'dash' (tip) in return for facilitating license and permit applications. This is an account of bribery in motion:

"I went to the Accra Metropolitan Office (AMA) at Adenta in Accra office one morning and was told to wait and meet the overall boss in charge of building permits. After waiting, this man came and gracefully walked into his office. Fifteen minutes later I was ushered into his office and I told him my mission. This building permit guy without even inquiring who I was or where I was coming from or who may have sent me asked me if I want an expedited building permit. I then asked him to explain himself further, whereupon he told me that if I want the permit within two days I have to pay 2,000 Ghana Cedis. He also told me that if I want it between three to four days I have to pay 1,500 Ghana Cedis but if I want it seven days it will cost me 1,200 Ghana Cedis. Please don't joke with this because it is a real story and I know the name of the official concerned. I then asked the AMA official if the levies he has mentioned were official levies and whether he was going to issue a receipt if I make the payment. The attitude of this man suddenly changed and he told me in the face that if I was not ready I should not subject him to any inquisition because he has other people waiting to see him."

As I was going towards my parked car I took the pains to talk to a low-level official of the AMA who told me that this is all what the man who is in charge of permit does. He daily robs people who go to the AMA office at Adenta to get building permits. I believe that there may be hundreds of people who have suffered at the hands of this seemingly corrupt AMA official"[83]. The relevance of political corruption is that it deprives corrupt politicians of the moral authority to use their powers in fighting corruption. We need to accept that no political party can fix this problem. But collectively, the citizens of Ghana and Africa can mount a credible challenge to this venality. As in Nigeria and many other African countries, Ghana's police are perceived to be among its most corrupt institutions. More than half of Ghanaian households perceive the police to be corrupt. Businesses believe Ghana's police services do not reliably enforce law and order. The traffic police are known to extract unofficial fees directly from drivers. Police officials in Ghana are criticized for corruption or negligence of their duties. Low salaries, which are sometimes not paid on time, contribute to police corruption. The Service has progressively grown into a ready instrument in the hands of the Administrator, which now uses it to hound and threaten their political opponents.

At Tema Port, custom officials demand bribes to release goods or allow illegal goods to enter the country. This practice is not indigenous to Ghana but endemic to all the nations in Africa. Complaints of corruption and harassment in relation to taxation are common, abuse of office, misapplication of exemption laws and political interference by the executive office is to name but a few. Amidst of all of this, Ghanaians are generally wary about blowing the whistle on corruption for fear of retribution and concern about their personal, family job security.

In 2016, Anas, an investigative journalist in Ghana, at a tremendous risk to self-harm exposed about thirty actively practicing judges for accepting bribes and fixing cases for such crimes as armed robberies. It is an understatement to say that the judicial system in Ghana is bankrupt and must be revamped to gain the confidence of the citizens. Although the tactics and procedures employed by Anas may be questionable, in some of these cases, illegal, it does not excuse the corrupt practices by which judgement is handed down. In Ghana and most African countries, justice is not blind; it is corrupt with capacious eyes. This is justice or injustice at the right price. Anas, is now traveling in Ghana incognito with disguises for his personal security. This avowal will resonate through-out this narrative, irrespective of the country in Africa.

L-R Kwame Nkuruma, Ignatius Kutu, Fred Akuffo Acheampong, Jerry Rawlings, J. J. Rawlings with CPT. Sankara and Dr. Limann

A legacy of political instability, insecurity and poor governance prevents the benefits of **Guinea**'s natural wealth from reaching the vast majority living in extreme poverty. Guinea's deteriorating reputation for corruption has threatened city services, choke economic growth and increase drug trafficking. The business and political cultures, coupled with low salaries, have historically combined to create and encourage a culture of corruption throughout Guinea's government system. Business is often conducted through the payment of bribes rather than by the rule of law. It is not uncommon for government officials to demand money for their personal use in exchange for favors or to just perform their duties.

In 2006, **Guinea** was perceived to be the fourth most corrupt country in the world. Guinea's lower rank is because of the dysfunctional administration, the weak judiciary, and embezzlement. Increasingly, drug traffickers have taken advantage of Guinea's poorly-staffed and meagerly -prepared justice system and easily-compromised public officials to transit drugs through Guinea to other West African countries, and on to Europe, making Guinea a trans-shipment hub for the transportation of illegal drugs coming from Brazil and other South American countries. To avoid any risk of arrest or imprisonment, the protection of a high-ranking army captain who will lend his help and name in the movement is sufficient, for drugs and drug pushers in Conakry. As in the other African countries, the residents of Conakry complain that the tentacles of corruption have suffocated everyday necessity like water supply, the delivery of electricity and relegated the health care system to service for bribe system. Young men, women and children die of preventable illness. Competent companies and individuals who can carry out projects are often brushed aside because they are not ready to pay or accept bribes. So, this leaves citizens with poorly-constructed roads and buildings, managed by incompetent people or those easily or willing to be compromised. With this degeneracy, Guinea continues to live with the unbearable corruption and poor infrastructure.[84] Guinea has vast mineral wealth, the world's largest reserves of bauxite and some of the highest grade iron ore deposits. Rendering these mineral resources productive for all Guineans, rather than a few deceitful nationals and international mining companies and politicians mean, challenging the deeply seated corruption in politics and business. But uprooting such corruption can be painfully slow, and is often very dangerous. This is no different from the rest of the countries in African continent.

An associate of Israeli billionaire Beny Steinmetz was jailed for two years after admitting that he attempted to obstruct a criminal investigation into allegations that Guinean government officials were paid bribes to award lucrative mining rights to the mogul. The rights to extract the iron ore at Simandou, situated in a mountainous region of Guinea's south-east, were unceremoniously stripped from Rio Tinto, and awarded to Beny Steinmetz Group Resources (BSGR). Cilins, a French national, was arrested in Florida as part of a US investigation into alleged illegal payments made to Guinean officials to secure mining rights for Steinmetz's BSG Resources. Frederic Cilins admitted to obstruct probe into allegations that government officials were bribed. Frederic Cilins, plead guilty after the FBI covertly recorded his conversations with Mamadie Touré, the widow of the former dictator of Guinea Mr Conté'. He was also fined $75,000 by a New York federal court.[85] Locals and Latin Americans long-accused of smuggling illicit drugs are operating freely in the country, some with high-level protection from within Conde's administration, according to Guinean and international law enforcement officials. "Whatever the attitude of the head of state, it's clear that traffickers can operate in Guinea."[86] In July 2014, Guinean anti-drugs agents were tipped off about a boat carrying cocaine. They scramble officers to the scene near Boffa, 80 km (50 miles) north of Conakry. They didn't get very far into the mission and were ordered off the case by another security forces. It was discovered later that the boat had been stripped of identification and communications equipment.[87] Drug trafficking in Guinea flourished in the years leading up to President Lansana Conté's death in 2008. In 2010, Mr. Alpha Condé, was pronounced winner of Guinea's first democratic election since the country gained independence from France in 1958, taking over from a military junta which had seized power in 2008 after Mr. Conté's death. Conté, the Guinean strongman who was the autocratic ruler of his country for almost twenty-five years after initially taking control as the head of the Military Committee for National Recovery (CMRN) that assumed power in April 1984, shortly after the death of Pres. Ahmed Touré. Dadis Camara, the army captain who seized power in the chaos after the end of Conté's twenty-four-year rule, hauled senior civilian and military figures before him to confess their roles in drug trafficking. The U.S. State Department report said officials tackling drug trafficking had been threatened due to their work. Dadis Camara fled Guinea after an assassination attempt in December 2009 by his Aide-de Camp.[88]

L-R, Ahmed Sekou Toure, Lansana Conté, Dadis Camara, and Alpha Conde

Burkina Faso is a landlocked country with weak industrial base, limited nature resources, high population density and very low adult literacy rate. About 90% of the population relies on agriculture to earn a living. In 1960, Burkina Faso gained independence from France. There have been several military coups between 1970s and 1980s'. Blaise Compaoré rose to power on 15 October 1987, by overthrowing and assassinating his predecessor and bosom buddy Thomas Sankara. With friends like this, who needs and enemy? It has been rumored that France encouraged the elimination of Sankara due to his economic and foreign policy decisions but there is no conclusive report to this fact.

Copious amount of the idolization that surrounds Sankara even after death. This adulation comes from a reputation for virtuousness in a continent of stupendously rich presidents, and from a self-confident position toward emancipation from western dependency. Upon assuming office, he quickly changed the name from Upper Volta to Burkina Faso, "the land of upright people." Really! After twenty-seven years in power, President Blaise Compaoré was suddenly ousted by a popular uprising on 30 October 2014, swiftly popped smoke and fled to Côte d'Ivoire.

The reason for the uprising was that Compaoré intended to amend Article 37 of the constitution, so that he could contest election for the presidency of Burkina Faso in 2015, which he was not entitled and continue his presidential messiah mandate. Other countries that have tried to scuttle the constitutional mandate are Nigeria, Burundi and Rwanda. It should be noted that Blaise Compaoré was a Soldier, coup leader and political godfather to Charles Taylor, the deposed and despotic president of Liberia. Compaoré may have played a key role in the destabilization of Côte d'Ivoire and the ousting of Ivorian president Laurent Gbagbo, who is currently awaiting trial at International Criminal Court at The Hague.

L-R Thomas Sankara with Fidel Castro of Cuba, Blaise campore

Like most African nations, **Mauritania** became an independent nation on November 28, 1960. Mauritania is probably the most racially segregated nation in Africa. This segregation has created ethnic strife and racial tension between Moors, Arabs, Berbers, and blacks. Although Mauritania officially abolished slavery in 1980, the nation continued to tolerate the enslavement of blacks by Moors, Arabs and Berbers. It is estimated that there were more than 90,000 chattel slaves in the country. In August 2005, President Taya was toppled by military officers while out of the country. In July 2008, the top four military juntas overthrew Prime Minister Boubacar and President Abdellahi in a bloodless revolution. Some of the same military leaders were involved in the 2005 coup that brought Abdellahi to power. Although progress has been made, laws and regulations are still not evenly and effectively enforced, largely because corruption has historically been so prevalent at every level of Mauritanian society and governmental affairs that it has been accepted as a normal way of life. The enslavement of black is still on-going.

Like the other African countries, corruption is an obstacle to direct foreign investment in Mauritania, but firms generally rate high taxes, access to credit, underdeveloped infrastructure, and a lack of skilled labor as greater impediments. Corruption is most pervasive in government procurement, bank loans, fishing license, land distribution, and tax payments. Giving or accepting a bribe is a criminal act punishable by two to ten years imprisonment and fines up to $700, but there is little application of this law. Firms commonly pay bribes to obtain faster telephone, electricity, water connections and construction permits.

Since assuming office, President Abdel Aziz has embarked upon a program to reduce privileges of government employees and to identify and punish those guilty of financial crimes. The current anti-corruption push began in November 2009 when the Bureau of Economic Crimes arrested the former governor of the Central Bank for alleged crimes committed between 2000 and 2001.

President Abdel Aziz arrest was quickly followed by the arrest of the former deputy governor of the Central Bank and the launch of an investigation into the business practices of twelve other prominent businessmen and bankers. The former Central Bank governor was accused of laundering approximately $95 million over the course of two years, the equivalent of nearly ten percent of Mauritania's 2010 budget. All of the individuals arrested in this first anti-corruption push were released in January 2010 and ordered to repay the entire amount. Without stiffer punishment such as incarceration, the citizens of Mauritania consider it an "old boys game" and the government not seriously concerned with fighting corruption.

Mauritania's Office of the Inspector General of the State handles financial investigations in the public sector. This agency, created in 2005, reports to the Prime Minister and has the authority to conduct investigations into all government offices and departments. From 2013-2014, there were four investigations and dismissals of senior governmental officers and managers of public institutions because of corruption or mismanagement.

The former Human Rights Commissioner was relieved of his duties and imprisoned in August 2010 on grounds of mismanagement. His trial concluded in December 2012 with time served, a $253,333 fine, and an order to reimburse $934,482 to the Mauritanian government. Mauritania has also reimbursed funds diverted under the previous administration from Global Fund programs intended to benefit those living with HIV/AIDS, and the international organization has now resumed support to the country.

These most recent investigations highlight the degree to which corruption in both the public and private sectors continues to occur. While most people do not doubt that the accused did in fact engage in corrupt practices, these investigations are controversial, as critics claim they are being conducted to settle old political scores. It is the doubt in such practices and political witch hunts that removes the credibility in the seriousness of battling corruption not just in Mauritania but in all of Africa.

Despite the current push to fight corruption, wealthy business groups and government officials reportedly receive frequent favors from authorities, such as unauthorized exemptions from taxes, special grants of land, and favorable treatment during bidding on government projects. Such widespread corruption has deprived the government of a significant source of revenue, weakening its capacity to provide necessary services.

Recent efforts to increase tax collection have proven controversial as business owners for the first-time face tax obligations that reflect the relatively high level of formal taxation for businesses that are not eligible for specialized exemptions. Tax collection efforts frequently incur criticism for their lack of procedural transparency.

There are several organizations that track corruption within Mauritania. Transparency International has a representative which reports on local corruption policies and events. Additionally, in 2008, several local nongovernmental organizations worked with a UN representative and the Mauritanian government to draft a National Action Plan to fight corruption. The plan was drafted and submitted in May 2010, but no anticorruption law has been issued by the legislature.[89]

L-R Sidi Ould Cheikh Abdallahi, Maaouya Ould Sid'Ahmed Taya, and Mohamed Ould Abdel Aziz

Chapter 3

East Africa

Uganda is a country with population estimated to be 27.2 million and majority of the populace live in rural areas. Uganda has witnessed one of the highest economic developments in Africa in recent years, yet challenges facing Uganda abound.

The current President of Uganda, Yoweri Kaguta Museveni, born 1944, in Mbarara district to cattle farmers. His cling to fame as a young boy was marauding cattle from near-by villages. Simply put, he was a cattle thief. This was a clue to what Museveni would become. He earned a B.A. in 1970 while studying political science and economics at the University of Dar es Salaam, in Tanzania. Museveni became chairman of a leftist student group allied with African Liberation Movements. When Idi Amin came to power in Uganda in 1971, Museveni went to Tanzania on a self -imposed exile.[90] There he founded the Front for National Salvation, making him a warlord. In 1979, successfully, with the aid of a former President and Prime Minister of Uganda, Milton Obote, they overthrew Idi Amin who swiftly fled to Saudi Arabia where he died naturally on the 19 of July 2003. A fate that was not accorded to many Ugandans. Idi Amin was known for his insatiable murderous rapt of the Ugandan people. It is considered that he caused the death of over 500,000 Ugandans. Some people speculate that the reason for his aberrant behavior is due to neurologic syphilis he contracted with his escapade and debauchery as a younger man but the more believable reason is that he suffered from untreated bipolar disorder, which manifested as quick-change and short violent temper;

being charming, happy, and charismatic one minute and then suddenly angry, violent, and brutal the next with little or no warning. Similar behavior was seen in Ghadaffi and Bokassa Later, Milton Obote was implicated in a gold smuggling plot, together with Idi Amin, then deputy commander of the Ugandan Armed Forces. When the Parliament demanded an investigation of Obote and the ousting of Amin, he suspended the constitution and declared himself President in March 1966, allocating to himself almost unlimited power under state of emergency rulings. Several members of his cabinet, who were leaders of rival factions in the party, were arrested and detained without charge.[91] After the overthrow of Milton Obote, Museveni marched his troops to Kampala and declared himself president of Uganda in 1986 and has been in power ever since.

In April 1997, the Ugandan government signed a purchasing arrangement for four helicopter gunships from Belarus. The helicopters were to be supplied by a UK-based company called Consolidated Sales Corporation (CSC). When the initial batch of two helicopters arrived in Uganda, however, they did not meet the specifications of the contract and turned out to be junk. The helicopters and the resulting lengthy dispute are estimated to have cost Uganda around $13 million USD. Major General Salim Saleh, the Minister of Defence at the time, confided in President Museveni, his eldest brother that CSC had offered him a bribe of $800,000 USD to help the deal go through. The contract price of each helicopter gunship was put at $1.5 million USD. Museveni ordered his brother to use the money to prosecute the war in northern Uganda. The inquiry discovered that Consolidated Sales Corporation never actually existed at the time when the supply contract was signed with the Ministry of Defense. It was registered in Uganda (as a foreign company operating on plot 8/10 Kampala Road) several months after the contract for the helicopters was signed. It was also revealed that while CSC had described itself as the seller and supplier of the helicopters, it was a mere broker with no direct links to the supplier in Belarus. It was established as a profiteering company that purchased the helicopters from Belarus through a series of middlemen, and in turn sold them for a hefty profit[92]. Museveni was elected to the post on May 9, 1996, and his backers won control of the National Assembly in legislative elections held the following month. Museveni was reelected in 2001 and again in 2006. Museveni is contesting for the Ugandan presidency again claiming that he is the only candidate with enough knowledge to address the affairs of

Uganda. As for his own future as leader of Uganda, Museveni told *Time:* "I'm not enjoying being president. I want to finish rebuilding the army, the police and the judiciary, and leave the country with a new constitution. And then I want to leave office."[93] In essence, he considers himself the savior of Uganda. If Museveni is not relishing being president of Uganda, why has he been in power for almost thirty years? Or, the people of Uganda love him this much for thirty years that he is continuously being elected as the president of Uganda. The main opposition candidate in Uganda's presidential election was arrested. Police detained Kizza Besigye at the offices of his Forum for Democratic Change party in the capital Kampala. Former Prime Minister Amama Mbabazi, who is the candidate for the opposition coalition, The Democratic Alliance (STD), issued a statement condemning what he called "the willful police brutality meted out against the FDC Presidential Aspirant, Dr. Kizza Besigye, and his colleagues. We call on Government to rein in the state police who have been brutalizing the innocent public.[94]

After a constitutional amendment passed the previous year that eliminated the established term limits for the presidency. He was reelected again in 2011, although the opposition and international observers noted obstructions with the polling process, this is a double talk to say that, the election was rigged in favor of President Museveni. In his foreign policy, Museveni often generated controversy by supporting rebels in other African countries. He backed Laurent Kabila, who deposed Mobutu Sese Seko in neighboring Zaire (now the Democratic Republic of the Congo) in 1997, the Tutsi exiles that were fighting against the government of Rwanda, and a group, headed by one of his former schoolmates and friend, Paul Kagame.[95] Museveni also came under fire for his lack of success with eliminating the Lord's Resistance Army (LRA), a militia led by Joseph Kony that terrorized northern Uganda and parts of central Africa for decades. Although the LRA was largely forced out of the country, the group continued to commit atrocities in neighboring countries.

Museveni justified his support of rebels stating that his goal was to achieve regional integration in both politics and economy and that the downfall of corrupt regimes was necessary to bring about such a union.[96] "He is the only one in the region who is not corrupt." This one time hero of Uganda has out lived his welcome. Bureaucratic and administrative forms of corruption are widespread in the Ugandan. Under Museveni's administration, with practices of bribery, nepotism, and misuse of official positions and resources is on the rise. Global Integrity estimates that half of the government's annual budget in 2006 was lost to corruption amounting to nine hundred and fifty million US dollars in spite of President Museveni's announcement of a zero tolerance for corruption. The government using public revenues to award enormous contracts to individuals who never supply the goods or the services contracted, in Uganda they call these unfulfilled contracts **'air supply'**. The organization gets the money and absconds, leaving the public with no projects or uncompleted project. It looks like Uganda is taking a trick from Nigeria's play book.

A former health minister in 2005 and a close supporter of Musevini and his deputies diverted two million dollars in fund provided by Global Alliance for vaccine for the vaccination and eradication of common childhood illnesses. In 2007, the government circumvented the proper contractual procedure for procurement and awarded a contract to a questionable company Kenlloyd Logistics to replenish Uganda's fuel reserve. The intrigue is the leader of this company is the son in law of the foreign minister who is related to the president.[97]

Thirty percent of Ugandans are of the opinion that government officials are engaged in corruption according to a 2005 survey by Afro Barometer. The World Bank Investment Climate Assessment undertaken in 2004, corroborates this finding with 46.3% of small firms and 56.5 % of mid-size firms identified corruption as a major or severe impediment to doing business in Uganda. This corrupt practice is not indigenous to Uganda, it is practiced throughout Africa. Firms typically make facilitation payments to speed-up bureaucratic processes, especially to obtain licenses, construction permits, Customs clearance, or simply to connect phone lines and electricity supplies. The scenario is, you may go to an office in the ministry and be told that your file cannot be located. Once the enablement money is made, your files will mysteriously appear.

United States Agency for International Development (USAID) survey identifies the lack of effective reporting systems, poor record management by state agencies, weakness of the judiciary, the poor investigation of corruption cases, and the lack of effective systems to punish corrupt officials, as major factors contributing to the high prevalence of corruption in public procurement. This is exactly the issues identified in Nigeria and the rest of Africa. [98] In 2003, five senior officers attached to the Large Taxpayer Department were involved in a major corruption scandal. A Commission of Inquiry of Corruption in the Uganda Revenue Authority (URA) was appointed by the government in the same year due to serious allegations of underestimated or misstated declarations in Customs, as well as collaboration between tax payers and Uganda Revenue Authority (URA) staff. The Commission released a much delayed and debated report two years later. But the legality was questioned by Members of Parliament. The report was ultimately nullified by the Ugandan High Court.[99]

The police were perceived as one of the most corrupt institutions in Uganda, particularly traffic police. Ninety-one percent of respondents to the 2005 Afro Barometer survey believe that the police are involved in corruption, while sixty-seven percent think that most or all police officials are involved in corruption. Only seventeen percent actually report having paid a bribe to avoid a problem or to get out of one with the police.[100] The reason for this low percentage is due to the fact that by reporting, you are essentially taking your life and the welfare of your family in your own hands. Investigations of police corruption have increased under the leadership of a police chief appointed in 2005. He has, however, faced internal criticism and has received several death threats.[101]

If this police commissioner is doing such a good job in curbing police corruption, who then is making threats against his life? Judges subsequently went on strike to protest against the invasion of the courts by security forces, and the East African Court of Justice found Uganda guilty of violating the rule of law and the rights of its citizens by allowing the military to repeatedly interfere with court processes. The Uganda Law Society noted that this episode reflected a broader problem of government officials refusing to comply with certain judicial actions.[102] According to the 2005 Afro Barometer, seventy-three percent of citizens think judges and magistrates are also involved in corruption, while the vast majority of citizens believe high level officials are significantly less likely to be held accountable for serious crimes than ordinary members of the public. Though past criticism has focused on an apparent reluctance to address corruption cases involving high ranking officials, the Inspectorate of Government (IGG) has lately taken a stronger stance, as demonstrated by the investigation of Solicitor General Lucien Tibaruha over alleged abuse of office. The IGG's effectiveness, however, has been hampered by a lack of qualified staff and sufficient funding. The US-Investment Climate Statement 2009 confirms these perceptions, reporting that several high-profile government corruption scandals have, in recent years, resulted in few or no sanctions against the officials involved.[103] As for freedom of association, freedom of speech and freedom of the press, these are guaranteed by the constitution are essentially nonexistent. Recently, however, the government has shown signs of growing intolerance towards independent media civil right organization, making homosexuality a punishable crime and has supported legislation restricting press freedom. There have also been instances where journalists have been selectively harassed or threatened when opposing the National Resistance Movement (NRM) officials. Uganda was the first country to conduct a Public Expenditure Tracking Survey in 1996. The survey showed that, on average, only Thirteen percent of annual capitation grants from the central government reached schools in 1991-1995. Eighty-seven percent were captured by local officials for purposes unrelated to education. In an attempt to remedy this, an information campaign was launched to educate local communities of their entitlements. The media campaign, combined with an increase in central government monitoring, reduced the diversion of funds by intermediary provincial governments from eighty to twenty percent.[104] "Gone are the days when you had to hide your car from greedy soldiers and carry cash in your pockets to pay them off when they stopped you."[105] This is encouraging but more still needs to be done to slow the erosion of Public confidence in government officials not just in Uganda but across Africa.

L-R, Milton Obote Idi Amin and Yoweri Moseveni

After the independence of **Kenya** in 1963 from Great Britain, Jomo Kenyatta assumed presidency and his mainly Kikuyu inner circle steadily plundered the country, ensuring that fellow Kikuyus and closely related Meru and Embu groups—together comprising some twenty-eight percent of Kenya's people—acquired an ever-larger slice of the land. In effect, a form of tribal supremacy. It has been rumored that the Kenyatta's family owns land the size of Belgium in the agriculturally rich part of Kenya. After Jomo Kenyatta death in 1978, his successor, Daniel Arap Moi, who hailed from the much smaller Kalenjin-speaking group of tribes, reckoned it was their turn to **"eat".** This is euphemism for amassing personal wealth and helping their families and friends to accumulate vast amounts of wealth at the cost of the nation, simply steal it any way you can because you may never get the chance again. Eventually, in 2002, in what looked like a pan-ethnic revolt against Mr. Moi's lost, Mr Kibaki, another Kikuyu, won a multiparty election amid hopes that Kenya would at last have a decent, reasonably clean administration in which merit rather than tribe would be the way to advancement. Mr. Githongo's appointment as the government's anti-corruption czar was hailed as a happy sign of such intent. No such luck. Mr Githongo almost immediately spotted a massive scam, involving murky company called **Anglo-Leasing,** that creamed off some $750m mainly by overbilling the state, with ministerial connivance in some eighteen projects. He noted that more than half of these scams had originated in Mr Moi's era but had deftly been carried over into the new and supposedly clean Kibaki administration. It soon became clear that not only were some of the most senior ministers in the government involved but also that the president was willing to look the other way. Moreover, as Mr Githongo made secret tapes of conversations with these scoundrels, two more things became equally clear. The main perpetrators, bound by a tight code of ethnic solidarity, flagrantly appealed to him, as a fellow Kikuyu to play ball, which is to be loyal to his tribe and the cause. He also realized, even after he had fled into self-imposed exile in England, that the this so-called "Mount Kenya Mafia" was determined to use some of its ill-gotten gains to fill party coffers in an effort to win the general and presidential elections due at the end of 2007. Money begets power and power more money. This group would stop at nothing to hold on to power.[106] "Ever since we started engaging our Chinese colleagues in business, transparency has crashed, and that is causing considerable concern vis-a-vis corruption and its potential implications with regards to governance problems." [107] Consider the proposal to build a standard-gauge railway from Mombasa to Nairobi and beyond. This project will cost $5.2 billion, it represents the biggest investment in Kenyan history and was awarded without public bidding process to a Chinese company blacklisted by the World Bank in 2009 for graft.[108] Is it any wonder how the Chinese company won the contract?

During Daniel arap Moi's presidency, corruption became rampart. In the 1990s, he was part of the Goldenberg scandal, where smuggled gold was exported out of Kenya in exchange for high government subsidies but the problem was **Kenya has no gold**. When the press and the courageous people of that country went over to Dubai and Switzerland to inspect the dummy corporations that supposedly received this gold, they found none. Mr. Moi and his cronies have wealth secreted abroad that is equal to the total national debt of Kenya. It's one of the largest corruption scandals to date in Kenya, which involved nearly the entire Moi government. Many officials from the Central Bank, and more than twenty senior judges have also been implicated. As of 2008, only a handful has been charged with criminal offenses, which some see as an example of the continuing problem of corruption and favoritism in Kenya.[109] On the economic front, this corruption caused a dramatic slide in the value of the Kenya Shilling and a large jump in the national inflation rate. The third president, Mwai Kibaki, was elected in 2002 mainly on the promise to end corruption in Kenya once and for all. Admittedly, there have been quite some improvements in the country (among them press freedom, return of elections and introduction of free and compulsory primary education for all) but corruption had remained. To start, his administration consists largely of Kikuyu, while this tribe is only twenty-two percent of the Kenyan population. From 2003 to 2006, Kibaki's cabinet spent 14 million dollars on new Mercedes cars for themselves. In late 2008, several members of Kibaki's parliament were found to have taken large "allowances", which were not legally part of their official compensation. And Kibaki probably manipulated the results of the 2007 election, leading to riots.[110] In the 2008 Corruption Perceptions Index, issued by the anti-corruption organization, Transparency International, ranked Kenya 147 out of 180 countries, meaning 146 countries are supposed to be less corrupt than Kenya, and 33 countries are more corrupt than Kenya. For comparison, the 180 country was Somalia whereas the first was Denmark. Corruption undermines the country's fledgling democracy by putting an unofficial price on all significant political positions that should under normal circumstances inform national policy. This widespread corruption has undermined public faith in national institutions and leadership.[111] Nearly forty-seven percent of the Kenyan population lives in absolute poverty that is concentrated among subsistence farmers, pastoralists, and people without any education and among unskilled workers. Corruption is considered an important cause of this poverty because it promotes unfair distribution of income and inefficient use of the nation's scarce resources.[112] The director of the Kenya Anti-Corruption Authority, Justice Aaron Ringera, revealed that a recent study by his institution found that, **presented with an opportunity to profit from corruption, a vast majority of Kenyans admitted they would jump at such an opportunity**.[113] Githongo squarely blames Mr Ringera for the government's failure to prosecute all the high ranking government officials implicated in the multi-billion shilling anglo-leasing scandal.[114] This was not very different from similar result found in Uganda and it may not be different in any other African country. This as a commentary is a sad, perverse state of affair. How does a country eradicate corruption since corruption is seen as a get rich quick scheme? It is only in Africa that governments have been periodically overthrown and their leaders lined up on the beaches facing a firing squad primarily for being corrupt. This is also the reason why they remain or try to remain in office as long as they can or die trying.[115] The virtue of Julius Nyerere, the former president of Tanzania is lost on the countries of East Africa. It is not for the want of laws because there are good laws on paper and impressive systems that are designed to be accountable and transparent but corruption has these laws in a death shroud.

Africa must start addressing the underlying social, political and economic rationales which facilitates corruption or it will continue to be marginalized by the world's elite and countries like China will plunder the natural resources, leaving empty holes in the ground to show for it and prosperity in China. It is uncertain why china should permit such questionable business practices in the continent of Africa when Chinese citizens go to jail when they engage in bribery and corruption in China. Some of the reasons why bribes are offered and accepted in Africa are policemen and civil servants take bribes because they cannot live on their derisory monthly salaries; and this is so true, businessmen who say that paying bribes is the only way to guarantee quick services from the government, in Swahili, it is called **"kito kidogo"** which means "something small" is the only way to win contracts. This was evident in Nigeria, Uganda and Kenya. This myopic view strangulates the country in the hands of few. In Kenya, and Africa in general, some of the largest contributors to the construction of churches and mosques in certain parts of the country and continent are individuals often mentioned in relation to cases of major corruption.[116] This may be a way for these pervert leaders to atone for their sins but more importantly, it is another way for these corrupt leaders to elevate and legitimize their status in the community, again by peddling influence.

There were times when the local school teacher, headmaster, chief, pastor and other such individuals were among the most highly regarded community leaders. In most parts of Africa, young men and women do emulated their headmaster or class teacher, now, a university diploma in Nigeria and other parts of Africa is not what the paper it is printed. This is because the entire education can be bought. This is known as **connection**. Responsive, accountable, transparent, and effective local government is a goal that many countries aspire to, but how is this achievable when nepotism, tribalism, cronyism, bribery and corruption have over taken moral righteousness. The only adjective that is not in play here is **racism**. Corruption at the local level undermines the delivery of basic services to residents and seriously challenge efforts to make democracy effective, safe and community vibrant.[117] Murungaru and colleagues pushed the idea that Githongo was a traitor, passing government secrets, an accusation Githongo denied. Such label carries a death penalty if found guilty. Realize that Chris Murungaru, the former interior minister whom Githongo had implicated in the Anglo-Leasing saga. Anglo-leasing scandal, which implicated people in Kibaki's government, was after his life just because Githongo was trying to eradicate corruption from his society. This is what Wole Soyinka, the Nigerian Nobel laureate in Corruption strikes back described as "those who are neck deep in the sewage of corruption ensure that they splatter sewage in all possible and improbable directions" because it is bound to touch someone. In other words, if I am going down I will take as many as I can. In Africa, you know something is amiss when a parallel crook accuses another crook of larceny. This is a case of kettle calling a pot black. The brazen, unchecked impunity of Kenya's political and business elite whether it comes to human rights violations or grand corruption remains one of the Kenya's and Africa's Achilles hill.[118] That level of liberty only encourages greater and greater corruption throughout Kenya at all levels. The resulting corruption has a direct impact on the business in the U.S., EU, Great Britain, etc.,attempting to operate in Kenya from the police roadblocks set up along major transport routes, to moving goods, to and from the Port of Mombasa, to fight counterfeit products that are undermining American manufacturers based in Kenya, and to simply being able to operate on a day-to-day basis with bribe-seeking local and regional officials. This narrative can be changed from Kenya to any other African country and the results will be the same. [119]

But why do so many African leaders cling to power even if it is detrimental to the interests of their countries? Some have argued that the post-independence model of Western democracy adopted by the African countries is alien to African culture. But this view is nonsense. Africa tends to be monarchical. Indeed, there are many African leaders with the mindset of ancient monarchs;

people who want to rule to eternity and then pass power to their sons. Show me a functional monarchy and I will show you a dis-functional society, where repression, human right abuse and corruption abound.

L-R Jomo Kenyatta, Raila Odinga , Daniel Arap Moi, Mwai Kabilai, Uhuru kenyatta and John Githongo (corruption Czar)

Chapter 4

Central Africa

The history of **Democratic Republic of Congo** has been one of civil war and corruption. After its independence from Belgium in 1960, the Republic of Congo (as it was then called) underwent five years of increasing civil tension. In1965, the dictator Lt. General Mobutu Sese Seko seized power and named the country Zaire and ruled the country for thirty-three years, with absolute power granted to him in the 1974 constitution.[120] The Democratic Republic of Congo is endowed with immense natural resources, and yet development of these resources has thus far failed to lift the majority out of abject poverty. The reason for this is Mobutu and the ruling elite looted the nation's resources to enrich themselves and their families. Mobutu, known for his trademark leopard-skin hat, amassed personal fortune estimated by Transparency International and others at between $1 billion and $5 billion, which he kept in Swiss banks. This was equivalent to the country's foreign debt at the time, and, by 1989, the government was forced to default on international loans from Belgium. This resulted in uncontrolled inflation, a large debt, and massive currency devaluations. Mobutu ruled by decrees and he almost crippled the economy through military spending, lack of financial oversight and poor monetary policies. Mobutu traveled by chartered Concorde and built a runway suitable for this plane to take off and land. The price for this flight is not for the faint of hearts. This is a plane that can fly at supersonic speed from London to New York in four hours. He and his family own sumptuous homes throughout Europe, including a sixteenth-century Spanish castle, a thirty-two-room Swiss chateau and a Brussels mansion called Fond de Roi, or Palace of the king. The evening news on television was preceded by an image of Mobutu appearing through clouds like a god descending from the heavens. Portraits of him adorned many public places, and government officials wore lapels bearing his portrait. He held such titles as "Father of the Nation," "Messiah," "Guide of the Revolution," "Helmsman," "Founder," "Savior of the People," and "Supreme Combatant." In the 1996 documentary of the 1974 Foreman-Ali fight in Zaire, dancers receiving the fighters can be heard chanting "Sese Seko, Sese Seko." At one point, in early 1975, the media was even forbidden from mentioning by name anyone but Mobutu; others were referred to only by the positions they held.[121]

Kabila, a long-time rival of Mobutu's and now president of Congo, began a military drive from eastern Zaire in October 1996 to depose him. Mobutu fled, first to Togo and then to Morocco. He had reportedly requested permission to travel to France for medical treatment, but the French government refused. Kabila now victorious with his entourage, political activists and adventurers from the Congolese diaspora in North America and Western Europe who had joined Kabila were appointed to high positions in government and other key institutions, in spite of their lack of experience and expertise. They quickly learned the ropes of how to benefit from their positions. Kabila's alliance with Uganda and Rwanda ended in August 1998. Both countries withdrew their troops to the eastern fringes of the DR Congo and from there, tried to re-conquer the country of Congo.[122] The country was again invaded for the second time by the same coalition. Kabila's regime was saved by support from Angola, Namibia and Zimbabwe. This divided the country into two, with the western half of the country remaining under the control of Kabila and his new allies (Angola, Zimbabwe and Namibia) and the northern and eastern fringes of the country being divided up among proxy warlords supported by Rwanda, Uganda and Burundi. Kabila's rule ended with his assassination in 2001. Kabila had given the order for his soldiers in the east to attack Goma in the eastern Congo, but the reality was that Congo's atrophied command-and-control system probably made the order impossible to enforce. In any case, local press quickly disclosed that $15 million meant for the army's sustenance had disappeared from the military's logistics section.[123] His son Joseph Kabila took over and immediately signed a peace deal with the various warring factions; he formed a transitional government in 2003.[124] Through all these political changes, corruption became ever more deeply entrenched into government systems, fueled further by civil wars and poverty. Self-enrichment by the political elite was perhaps encouraged by lack of certainty of how long peace would prevail. Several reports mention that army generals past and present are grabbing mineral-rich land and privately negotiating with foreign investors for mining concessions.[125]

The development of Congo is underpinned by their conviction that improvements in infrastructure necessitate regional integration, enables intra-regional trade, connects regions to global market and attracts private sector investment. This was one of the underlying reasons why IMF supported the Inga Dam scheme. The construction and operation of this megaproject was beset by corruption. The Multilateral Development Banks' Working Group on Infrastructure finds that "mismanagement and corruption contributed to significant losses estimated at ten to thirty percent of project's value during construction projects.[126] The 2012 Transparency International's Corruption Perception Index for DRC ranked 160 out of 179 countries. The construction sector leads the world's hit-list of corruption-prone activities. Customs agents, police and government officials asked for a bribe **"un petit sucré,"** which is literally, in the Congolese parlance, "a little soft drink or something sweet"[127] The Democratic Republic of Congo is no stranger to this practice. In any language, especially, French, corruption is not romantic or sweet.

Despite this regulation, there have been reports of cases (especially in the mining and oil sectors) where contracts were awarded in secret, without a tender process. A good case in point was raised by the Financial Times concerning Dan Gertler; a businessman close to the Congolese President. Mr. Gertler is held to be one of the main partners in two offshore companies that obtained oil blocks in north-eastern DRC under controversial circumstances.[128] Dan Gertler obtained their licenses after the government cancelled licenses for the same blocks that had been attributed to other firms. The reason why this company was chosen as the new license-holder to the oil blocks remains unclear. Dan Gertler is said to have no known track record in the oil industry and it is presumed that his company Caprikat is registered in the British Virgin Islands.[129] It is not uncommon to hear of engineering firms bribing their way through the contract award phase of infrastructure development projects in developing countries using **political patronage** and **clientelism.** This involves the siphoning of public resources to sustain a web of patronage networks that helped in acquiring the mega contract. Political patronage and clientelism in the DRC is reflected by the overrepresentation of individuals close to the President or the cabinet. These political sycophants are seen in Nigerian Presidents Jonathan, Olusegun Obasanjo, and General Buhari, Mobutu Sese Seko etc administrations and all over Africa. Corruption in the DRC is widespread through all levels of society. Police said they are investigating allegations that former prime minister Adolphe Muzito enriched himself from public funds. It is alleged that the ex-prime minister owns more than 100 houses and apartment buildings, including buildings in New York and apartments in Washington. He also said Muzito owned an aviation company, Banair, which was a joint venture between Technafrique, a company he put in his wife's name.[130] A 2008 report by Global Integrity stated that inefficient government structures, low salaries and an absence of oversight provide civil servants with opportunities and incentives for extorting money from the population.[131] Société Nationale d'Electricité (SNEL), the country's national utility company has been fraught with problems for decades. During the Mobutu years, it failed to collect electricity tariffs from government entities, residential users and mining companies. SNEL is currently unable to provide electricity to all of Kinshasa because of low production levels at the Inga I and II dams because of the aged, poorly maintained state of its transmission lines. As a result, SNEL only provides power during specific time slots to different neighborhoods, leaving portions of the capital without power for days and weeks this is the same sad irony found in Nigeria. Power disruption due to damaged transmission lines are common, but it has been reported that they are sometimes provoked by SNEL technicians who then receive bribes to repair the lines or reconnect the customer to the power grid. [132] SNEL has been linked with grand corruption scandals as well. In 2008, two of SNEL's top directors were interrogated after the disappearance of $6.5 million US ear-marked for Inga II rehabilitation. The money was never recovered or accounted. Recently the Chinese consortium Sicomines landed a $6.5 billion megadeal in exchange for mining copper and cobalt with Congo's state mining agency. The Chinese Sicomines deal is of concern in that the DRC government has no studies that estimate the potential value of the minerals at the site and also that there was a 'signing bonus' of $350 million whose recipient is not publicly known. This similar to the deal Kenyan government went in to with the Chinese cataloged in John Githongo's chronicles. It is also clear that all efforts to reign in corruption on the African continent have not improved the situation but perhaps have made the corruptee and corruptor more sophisticated than before. [133] A combination of extortion and badly targeted taxation was preventing the creation of small businesses which are the lifeblood of economies and employment in most countries. Poor government and corruption have hindered Congo's economic progress and hampered efforts to tackle massive unemployment. As a contribution to restoring the DRC's debt sustainability, the Paris Club creditors will provide a cancellation of $7.35 billion USD, fulfilling all their commitments under the enhanced HIPC initiative. Paris Club creditors expressed their concern over the business environment and urged the Government of the DRC to carry out further reforms to improve governance, strengthen the rule of law and fight corruption. Successive United Nations investigations have accused the coterie of officials around Kabila of plundering state-owned diamond companies and other natural treasures.

L-R Mobutu Sese Sekou Joseph Kabila Laurent Kabila

Since Burundi became an independent country on July 1, 1962, there has been series of unfortunate violence along ethnic lines. It has become a constant way of life in Burundi. In September 1972 between 200,000 and 300,000 lost their lives and possessions. Significant number Hutus were killed and another 300,000 fled into exile. Sixteen years later, some 150,000 Hutus were massacred again, in clashes with the army. The economy has declined and coup d'état have been frequent and the competition for power along tribal lines. Burundi's economy is one of the world's poorest, landlocked and devoid of any significant natural resource of export except tobacco.

The 1993 assassination of President Melchior Ndadaye led to a decade civil war which the February 28, 2005 the Constitution tried to resolve. Since corruption and all sorts of abuses of power grew exponentially, many Burundians discuss corruption as being the result of the war. While this is false, it safe to say that corruption occurred pre-war but the impact and magnitude is in the fore front. Ordinary Burundians knew how the system worked, how to behave in order to solicit benefits (though in theory as citizens they had rights to those benefits), how to connect to the more powerful, how to donate little gifts to get things done.[134] This image testifies to the general sense that corruption has changed in nature and volume during those years. It was under the constitution of the then Good Governance Minister, Pierre Nkurunziza became president for a five-year tenure. At war's end, a number of new dynamics were added to the previous ones. First, total international aid increased dramatically. A lot of the new international funding went to reconstruction and rehabilitation projects such as roads, bridges, hospitals, schools, as well as continued emergency aid for food, return of the citizens that fled Burundi during the war re-settlement and shelter, etc. These projects were cash cows for the corrupt, providing almost endless opportunities for illicit gain.[135] A lot of money could be made by those without scruples and with good connections. More than fifty percent of the funds of major bilateral and multilateral donors frequently disappear without trace.

Pierre Nkurunziza has been at the helm of Burundian government for ten years. This former college lecturer has dubiously forgotten almost everything about serving the people. Nkurunziza was re-elected five years later for a final second term, now he insists on a Third Term. His reason is that it was the Parliament, not the general electorate that elected him president for his first term. Nkurunziza may be technically right in his argument nevertheless morally wrong for a Third Term presidential bid, but is it worth so much bloodshed and instability to his country? Is his selfish ambition worth the lives of Burundians? One reason why leaders like Nkurunziza fester on the African continent is the lack of Social Movements comprising of the workers, students, conscientious intellectuals and other progressive forces that can bring pressure to bear on any African leader irrespective of nation or origin.[136] While the rest of the world throw their hand in the air and say it is not our problem. Yet after the blood bath, some will quickly send aid in form of donation which will be squandered as fast as it is given. Since the failed coup, President Nkurunziza has set out to settle scores with his identified enemy besides, ordinary citizens are paying the price. In Burundi, as elsewhere in Africa, centrally-instigated violence spreads through the country by feeding into local conflicts and grievances. Corruption and its corollary, lack-of-rule and of law, creates a multitude of local points of contention, sense of exclusion and abuse, lingering angers at past abuses and grievances and the need to avenge old wrongs. This vicious circle increases the risk for new dynamics of violence to take root in tribal wars in Burundi.[137]

Nkurunziza's refusal to accept Peace Keeping Troops authorized by African Union is a sign of looming disaster, the declaration of such occupation force without invitation will quickly position the country to civil war. The outcome of this posturing will determine the future for Burundi and President Nkurunziza to a greater extent, the African Union.

As corruption now prevails under a blatantly Hutu-dominated regime, it becomes increasingly clear to people that it is not the system that is at fault not the Tutsi or Hutu but the individuals in government. Certainly, many intellectuals have started seeing it that way. This may lay the basis for non-ethnic coalitions of anger for political change, if credible and non-corrupt political entrepreneurs manage to emerge in Burundi.[138] This is the catalyst the citizens of Burundi need to truly transform their nation. The police generally are poorly trained, underequipped, underpaid, and largely unprofessional. They are widely perceived by local citizens as corrupt and are often implicated in criminal activity, including bribery. Approximately seventy-five percent of the police force were former rebels; Eighty-five percent had received minimal entry-level training and no refresher training in the past five years, and fifteen percent had received no training yet they are called police officers. Due to low wages, petty corruption is widespread. Police officials have been implicated in cases of torture, human right abuses, rape and extrajudicial execution. The government's general reluctance and slowness to investigate and prosecute these cases result in a widespread perception of police ineptitude and impunity.[139]

In spite the tragic and violent past, **Rwanda** is fast becoming the most transparent country in Africa. Rwanda is now the safest, cleanest country in Africa, with no slums and virtually no begging, pan handling or street crime. Twenty-two years after the genocide in which Hutu fanatics premeditated the carnage of more than 800,000 Tutsis and moderate Hutus, leaving the country a nightmarish ruin and corpses stuffed down the wells. Local rivers and stream filled with bloated bodies of Hutu atrocities. People taking shelter in churches were not spared. Despite Rwanda's humble beginning, corruption is still wide spread and systemic in the country. After all, it is still an African state. It was reported that thirty-five percent of the corruption cases involved public fund embezzlement or illegal transfer of district natural resources and resource mismanagement by district leaders and their assistants. And about thirty percent of these cases were prosecuted in 2004 according to Transparency International a watch dog that monitors national corruption. The Police have been implicated in several incidences of corruption. About one hundred and thirty-nine were fired in 2004 and additional eighty were sacked in 2005. The current ruler of Rwanda Paul Kagame, grew up in a refugee camp in Uganda, having fled there with his parents at the age of three. It was 1961 and the Rwandan Hutus were engaged in a war of independence from the Belgians. At eighteen, Mr. Kagame went into the bush, as did hundreds of other young Rwandan men, to join a Ugandan rebel force led by Yoweri Museveni, now the President of Ugandan. When the Museveni forces became the Government, Mr. Kagame remained in the army and became Head of intelligence. He went to the United States in the fall of 1990 for a course at the Army's Command and General Staff College in Fort Leavenworth, Kansas, one of US Army premier military institute responsible for training and doctrine in US Army to complement what he had learnt in Cuba. Kagame and Rwigyema continued to plot their invasion by telephone, as the Ugandan military became increasingly suspicious of the Rwandans in their midst He cut his studies short and rushed the RPF, detached himself from the Ugandan Army, ripped the insignias off its uniforms, and crossed the border into Rwanda. By the time Kagame got there, Rwigyema had been killed, and the RPF had been routed. At thirty-three years, he took command of the Rwandan Patriotic Front after the death of their commander Fred Rwigyema. He went on to stabilize and improve the country. Kagame, the president of Rwanda, is considered to be the most dynamic and effective leader in Africa today. There is a national health system, nineteen out of twenty children are in school, while still in severe poverty, has better internet service than rural Britain, and a good network of immaculately paved and roads.[140] Unlike most African warlord that transitioned in to civilian leadership, Kagame doesn't appear motivated by wealth or luxury, either for himself or his relations. Rather the mineral wealth appears to have been funneled through government channels, with most of it spent on the military, and the rest of it helping to finance Kagame's vision of an African Singapore. It is particularly troubling that Paul Kagame is seeking a third term in office as the president of Rwanda contrary to Rwanda's constitutional mandate of two terms for the presidency. The dangerous precedent set by Kagame will embolden others after his departure from office to contest for a third term in office if the constitution is not amended. Although it is beyond the scope of this book to discuss human right abuses, Kagame has been directly implicated in the killing of his intelligence chief in South African Hotel. This is an allegation he denies but said that anyone who is a traitor to his country is worthy of assassination.

The **Central African Republic** embarked on its independence from France under challenging circumstances in the leadership of President David Dacko. Upon his return from military assignment in France, Bokassa quickly rose through the military ranks and was named Army Chief of Staff by President David Dacko, his cousin, in 1964. Like Idi Amin of Uganda, Bokassa, a former Soldier in French Army and saw action in Algeria and Indonesia.

On January 1, 1965, Bokassa named himself President after a successful military coup toppling his cousin. It is all in the family. He announced on the radio, saying, "The hour of justice is at hand. The bourgeoisie is abolished. A new era of equality among all has begun. Central Africans, wherever you may be, be assured that the army will defend you and your property." This promise to the people of Central African Republic never came to fruition. This revolutionary massage meant that Bokassa will defend himself and steal your property. This is also when the problems of Central African Republic really began. Within months of taking power Bokassa invalidated the constitution and replaced the National Assembly with a Revolutionary Council. With an abundance of arable land, rainfall, a plethora of minerals and wildlife and a low population, the Central African Republic (CAR) should be a wealthy nation by any standard. The country's rich uranium and diamond deposits helped Bokassa gain favors from both France and the United States, but failed to put much money into the nation's treasury. Bokassa's extravagant lifestyle kept the Central African Republic on the verge of bankruptcy. In April 1969, Minister of State Alexandre Banza, who had participated in Bokassa's coup, led his own takeover attempt. The coup failed, and Banza was subsequently executed for treason. Bokassa promoted himself to full General in 1971, then to Marshal and President-For-Life in March 1972. He survived another coup attempt in December 1974 and narrowly avoided an assassination attempt in February 1976. In September 1976, with public dissent growing and international support waning, Bokassa dissolved the government and replaced it with the Conseil de la Révolution Central Africaine (Central African Revolutionary Council). Hoping to gain much-needed financial and military aid from Libyan despotic leader COL Muammar al-Gaddafi, Bokassa converted to Islam and changed his name to Salah Eddine Ahmed Bokassa. IF THIS IS NOT SERIOUS, IT WILL BE COMICAL. This change of heart conversion to Islam did not last, however, as the implied aid never came, he quickly re-converted back to Catholicism within three months. Situation in Central African Republic went from bad to worse. On December 4, 1976, he instituted a new constitution that renamed the country the Central African Empire and proclaimed himself Emperor. It is said that the profligate coronation formality consumed the nation's entire annual budget. It was estimated that coronation cost $20 million, which was a third of the country's total budget and France's entire aid for the year. On September 20, 1979, France sent a Corps of Paratroopers into the Central African Republic, which forced Bokassa to resign, and David Dacko was restored to the presidency.[141] Jean-Bédel Bokassa died of a heart attack on November 3, 1996, and was buried in the village of Berengo area of Central African Republic. Bokassa's mental instability is eerily similar to the mental maladjustment seen in Idi Amin Dada of Uganda and COL Gaddafi of Libya.

Civilians in the Central African Republic have been the victims of ongoing violence and human rights violations in the wake of brutal sectarian warfare. In October 2002, former Army Chief of Staff Francois Bozize launched a coup d'état coup attempt that culminated in the March 15, 2003 overthrow of President Patasse and the takeover of the capital. Bozize, who was Chief of Staff of the Army under Patasse, was implicated in ordering the killing of several anti-Kolingba rebels in Kembe Prefecture in 1999. Bozize was thought to have liquidated a small, select group of Patasse sympathizers after his 2003 coup, but this was targeted and short in duration. President Bozize's kleptocratic government appeared content to control Bangui, the wood and diamond reserves of the southwest, and other isolated regions with diamond, uranium and mineral deposits in the east. From this, they were able to steal enough money to buy large properties in Burkina Faso and South Africa, France and live comfortably. General Bozize in his uniforms adorned with shiny epaulettes and brass buttons declared himself President, suspended the constitution, and dissolved the National Assembly.

General Bozize and the other African leaders view the military as both a guarantor of their power and a threat because a coup d'état may happen anytime and their regime overthrown. Diamond smuggling and corruption touch the highest levels of the CAR. In 2004, about a year after he came to power in a coup, President Bozize's supporter was briefly detained in a German airport with a briefcase full of diamonds. Many political figures pay for artisanal miners to dig diamonds or simply buy the diamond from local miners. Under the disguise of official travel, these crooks carry the precious stones to Europe particularly Antwerp, Belgium where they are then peddled.[142] It is a well-known fact that Antwerp, Belgium is a place were smuggled diamonds and other precious stones are easily fenced. The musical chairs of coup and counter coup continued in Central African Rebulic.

In March 2013, former President Francois Bozize was ousted from power and forced to flee after Seleka led, mostly muslim rebel force, led by Michel Djotodia took over large parts of the country. To counter this, the Christian anti-Baleka formed in response to Seleka hits, and reprisal attacks followed. Michel Djotodia seized power as the leader of the Seleka movement in March 24, 2013 toppling President Bozize. France sent forces to control the violence in December 2013, and a U.N. peacekeeping force was deployed in September 2014. Djotodia stepped down early in 2014 and left the country after failing to stop sectarian violence by his Seleka rebels and was replaced by interim President Cathrine Samba Panza, the first and one of three female presidents of African nation. In Central African Republic, it is rumored that individuals can buy hand grenade for the price of soft drink, mostly Chinese made. If this is correct, the only people profiteering are the Chinese at the cost of human lives. Corruption, poverty and the lack of sustainable infrastructure like every other African nation is thwarting Central African Republic from flourishing. In the end, Corruption remains pervasive in Central African Republic. Armed groups engage in the illicit trade and exploitation of natural resources—especially wild life, gold and diamonds—which account for more than half of export earnings further impoverishing a population of 4.6 million.[143]

L-R Bokassa, Djotodia, Bozize, Patasse and Cathrine Samba Panza

Chapter 5

South Africa

The British Government formally granted independence to **Zimbabwe** on April 18, 1980. Prime Minister Mugabe's policy of reconciliation was generally successful during the country's first two years of independence, as the former political and military opponents began to work together. In 1981, several MPs from Ian Smith's party the former administrator of Zimbabwe left to sit as "independents," signifying that they did not automatically accept his anti-government posture. More importantly, government security officials discovered large caches of arms and ammunition on properties owned by ZAPU, and Joshua Nkomo, the former prime minister, and his followers were accused of plotting to overthrow Mugabe's government. Nkomo and his closest aides were expelled from the cabinet.

Opposition to President Mugabe and the ZANU-PF government has grown in recent years, in part, due to worsening economic and human rights conditions. The opposition, currently led by Morgan Tsvangiari and the Movement for Democratic Change (MDC), was established in September 1999.

The MDC's first opportunity to test opposition to the Mugabe government came in February 2000, when a referendum was held on a draft constitution proposed by the government. Among its elements, the new constitution would have permitted President Mugabe to seek two additional terms in office, grant government officials immunity from prosecution, and authorize government seizure of white-owned land. The referendum was handily defeated. Shortly thereafter, the government, through a loosely organized group of war veterans, sanctioned an aggressive land redistribution program often characterized by forced expulsion of white farmers from their land and violence against both farmers and farm employees. Transparency International's (TI) 2010 Corruption Perception Index (CPI), which measures the degree to which corruption is being perceived in 178 countries around the world, ranks Zimbabwe on 134 position. It is reported that it would take Zimbabwe, at present-day configuration, 190 years to double its $600 GDP per capita. Today, the Zimbabwean dollar has been discarded in favor of the United States dollar and the Reserve Bank of Zimbabwe has also accepted the South African rand, Botswana pula, pound sterling, euro, Chinese Yuan, Australian dollar, Indian rupee and Japanese yen as legal tender. Any other currency but Zimbabwean dollar.

A classic case of corruption was where the city authorities sold twenty-six commercial properties of which only six were sold through proper procedures (Manyukwe, 2010, p. 1). Manyukwe stated that the other twenty were allegedly sold clandestinely by former Mayor Marange and the Town Clerk. There is further mention of the Minister of Local Government Rural and Urban Development in the selling of the twenty, with the Minister getting land to build a hotel. Chitungwiza Municipality officials were alleged to have allocated in-fill stands in a manner that was riddled with corruption, with the waiting list at the council not being followed. These stands were offered to those who could afford to bribe council officials.

Council officials tend to give preference to those who are able to offer bribes due to shortage of vending spaces. The citizens for their part seem to accept that paying bribes is the normal way of getting services from the council.

In 2011, finance minister Tendai Biti claimed that at least $1 billion in diamond related revenue owed to the national treasury remains unaccounted. This issue is particularly critical as such practices militate against the council's efforts to create employment in the informal sector and thus alleviate poverty while at the same time increasing the municipality's revenue base.

Nursery schools are expected to be leased by council to capable individuals or organization. However, the nursery schools were being controlled by either former Zimbabwe African National Union Patriotic Front (ZANU PF). These politicians are allegedly taking advantage of the council's laxity in monitoring and thus not paying rentals to the council. This does not only deprive the council from the much needed revenue but it will also deny other members of the community an opportunity to participate in potential income generating activities.

There is illegal conversion of land space earmarked for community development projects such as recreational facilities, schools, and business to residential stands. The process is alleged to involve both politicians and public officials in the municipality. Tenders for repairing the municipality's fleet of vehicles were awarded to a private company called Glatifin which is linked to high ranking political officials in the municipality. There are also other instances where former councilors, appointed officials and private contractors collude to strip the council of its assets.

Things began falling apart in Zimbabwe around the year 2000 when Mugabe decided to accelerate the process of land redistribution by forcibly seizing holdings. To be sure, the pattern of land ownership was historically highly iniquitous in Zimbabwe, and some land reform was definitely needed. Mugabe sought approval and admiration by a controversial land reorganization program, whereby white farmers were forcibly disinherited of their farms and handed over to his influential supporters, judges, army officers, etc. This effort at land redistribution sent the economy into freefall. Zimbabwe went from the bread basket of southern Africa to the basket case of Africa. Zimbabwe currency became worthless to the point that one can buy a loaf of bread with one million Zimbabwe dollars. Inflation in Zimbabwe is an unbelievable 1,700 percent a year. An estimated 80 percent of the working-age population is unemployed. Basic foodstuffs and fuel are unavailable. Zimbabweans began to flee the country in droves to places like South Africa. Zimbabwe has had more than its fair share of scandals involving parastatals and public offices. The GMB, Zinwa, Noczim, Air Zimbabwe, Ziscosteel, Arda and NRZ have all been defrauded to bankruptcy by public officials. The corrupt officials running those organizations have, at worst been transferred and there has been no serious effort to prosecute them or recover what they have prejudiced against the State. Mugabe has plundered state assets such as Air Zimbabwe, which he uses as his personal airline, regularly diverting scheduled flights to accommodate his Vasco Da Gama-esque penchant for foreign luxury travel. Agricultural and Rural Development Authority is now treated as the personal property of Mugabe. Numerous reports have surfaced about Mugabe's stolen billions stashed away in Asian bank and Properties in Hong Kong, Singapore and South Africa.

A small monarch in the southern region of Africa, **Swaziland**'s average life expectancy is the lowest in the world, at thirty-three years and nearly seventy percent of its citizens live on less that one dollar a day. Greater than forty percent are unemployed but King Mswati lives lavishly, using the kingdom's treasury to fund expensive taste in German automobiles. This gross mis-management of Swaziland's finances has caused a collapse of the economy leading to the disintegration of the nation's pension fund also the withdrawal from 2013 African Cup of Nations. The next step will be for Swaziland to request for international aid or forgiveness of outstanding loans relative to gross misappropriation of scarce national resources the most unfortunate situation is the unavailability of national resources to earn foreign reserve except tobacco cultivation.

Joshua Nkomo, Bishop Abel Muzerewa , Robert Mugabe and Morgan Tsvangiari

The history of **South Africa** is checkered because of the repressive practices of apartheid. Substantial proportion of modern corruption occurs in regional administrations this, certainly embodies a legacy from the homeland civil services. A major source of financial misappropriation in the old central government, secret defense procurement, no longer exists but corruption is stimulated by new official practices and fresh demands imposed upon the bureaucracy including discriminatory tendering, political solidarity, and the expansion of citizen entitlements.[144] Jacob Zuma the president that succeeded Tabo Mbeki is being probed by South African police for alleged corruption linking him to $24m state-funded upgrade of his house including the construction of a swimming pool, private clinic and amphitheater. Zuma has faced both political and public wrath of the excessive spending, in a country battling rampant unemployment and inequality. South Africa has invented its own vernacular on corruption for example **Tenderpreneurism** which describes individuals who enrich themselves through perverting the awarding of government tender contracts, mostly based on personal connections and corrupt relationships, unmitigated bribery also take place, sometimes these shameful practices involve elected or politically appointed officials. Another one of these vernaculars is **BEE-fronting** which is an abuse of the rules governing Black

Economic Empowerment (BEE), where qualifying persons are given a seat on the Board of Directors of a company while having no decision-making power in the company, in order to qualify the company for government contracts.

In 1999, the South African government announced its largest-ever post-apartheid arms deal, signing contracts totaling 30bn rand ($5bn; £2.5bn) to modernize its national defense force. The deal involved companies from Germany, Italy, Sweden, Britain, France and South Africa. In 2005, Jacob Zuma was sacked as South Africa's deputy president after his financial adviser, Schabir Shaik, was convicted of fraud and corruption.[145]

Shaik was found guilty of trying to solicit a bribe from Thint, the local subsidiary of French arms company Thales, on behalf of President Zuma.

The prosecution alleged that, in exchange, President Zuma was to shield the firm from an investigation linked to the 1999 deal. Shaik said the money was a donation to the Jacob Zuma Education Fund. Sure! Shabir Shaik, advisor to then Minister of Tourism and later Deputy President of South Africa, Jacob Zuma, arranged the payment of various expenses and debts owed by President Zuma through several of his companies. Shaik also solicited business joint ventures on the basis of his political access from this arrangement as well as procuring bribes to generate additional funding for Zuma which were also laundered through a series of companies held by a prolific South African business man.[146]

Shaik was also convicted of paying R1.3m to President Zuma in bribes to use his influence to further Shaik's business interests. The fraud count related to the accounting of the payments. Shaik is currently serving a fifteen-year sentence and was ordered to pay $5.5m of his assets to the state. Another official, Tony Yengeni, who was the chairman of parliament's defense committee at the time of the deal, was convicted of fraud in 2003.[147] The Department of South Africa's Home Affairs says it's arrested twenty-six of its own officials for corruption and fraud since July this year. Their crimes include the issuing of fake identity documents and attempts to solicit bribes from applicants at local offices.

President Olusegun Obasanjo's government had allocated South Africa the right to market 55,000 barrels of Nigerian crude a day in government-to-government contract that was a first between the two countries. The pretense that this oil allocation was to be handled by the government of South Africa for the benefit of the people of South Africa. However, neither the oil, nor the revenue, was to come to South Africa. Another falsehood was being perpetuated at the time: Nigeria, then only six months into the civilian administration of Obasanjo, said it would cut the corruption that characterized its lifeblood oil industry. Under previous military dictatorships many crude, lifting contracts had gone to cronies, at a substantial discount, who sold their allocations at market rates. They split the margin between themselves and their politico-military patrons. Africa Confidential, under the headline "Cleaning up oil", explained: "Under previous governments, crude sales were a fountain of political patronage, as military officers and politicians sponsored traders' bid for contracts." Out of such deals the 'sponsor' could earn as much as five [US] cents a barrel, which added up nicely when some sponsors controlled more than 70,000 barrels a day. The commission system may have cost the NNPC [the state oil company, the Nigerian National Petroleum Corporation] as much as $1.5-billion a year. What Obasanjo's government and the NNPC did to "clean up" the oil industry in July 1999 was to cancel all forty-one lifting contracts awarded by the former military regime and announce a "transparent" process to award new contracts. These new contracts, the state oil company said, would cut out the crony intermediaries. To qualify, bidders had to be "bona fide end-users that is, companies that owned their own refineries" or recognized "large volume traders. Qualifying bidders would also have to show commitment to Nigeria by investing in community development or the energy sector. When the NNPC announced the successful candidates for the new one-year "term contracts", as they are called, in August 1999, thirteen well-known refiners and traders were included. Three countries that would get "government-to-government" contracts and it was widely reported as such also on the list: Kenya, Ghana and South Africa. In Kenya and Ghana, the successful bidders were reportedly their national oil companies. In the remaining case, the recipient was noted simply as "South Africa". As it turned out, the "South African" recipient would fall into none of the above categories. It was not an end-user, and it was not a recognized large volume trader; it was not a government. Certainly, the state and the people of South Africa were not to benefit.[148]

In **Zambia**, eighty-seven percent of the general population perceives corruption to be a problem in the country with the growing tendency for government officials to demand bribe in return for services performed. Independent since 1964, Zambia has experienced five successful multiparty elections since the return to multiparty politics in 1991. President Mwanawasa confirmed in February 2007 that about six million euros was stolen from the government by public servant in four years. Fredrick Chiluba, the former President and former Zambian ambassador to US and former intelligence chief, and many others were found liable for defrauding the government in the tune of forty-one million dollars by London high court. Persistent petty corruption involving the police, the court system and other government parastatals services could only be accomplished in exchange for unofficial payment similar to the rest of African countries this is not particularly unique to Zambia. The Anti-Corruption Commission arrested Mwanawasa's press aide Arthur Yoyo in late 2002 and charged him with corruption and abuse of office before he was suspended from his position pending his court case. The arrests are independent of those by an anti-corruption task force, set up by Mwanawasa to probe the affairs of former president Frederick Chiluba, who faces various charges of corruption, theft and abuse of office amounting to about $45 million.

Former military commander, Wilford Funjika, was arrested and charged with corruption for allegedly engaging in illegal business deals while serving under Chiluba. A former press aide to President Richard Sakala was jailed for five years by the magistrates' court for theft of government vehicles and properties, abuse of office and corruption.

There is high risk for companies to encounter petty corruption with Zambia's police. Corruption is fueled by an abnormal degree of liberty, a lack of professional training, and low salaries. Extortion is common at roadblocks, when processing documents, and commencing investigations. Zambia's police are perceived as a corrupt organization, having demanded the largest amount of bribes among all public institutions in 2014. Corruption takes place in eight out of ten interactions with the Zambian police (ZBPI 2014). Due to the poor reliability of police services to protect businesses against corruption and fraud, companies identify the business costs of crime to be high. The level of Judicial independence is low and decreases competitiveness of the business environment. Local courts deal with a huge backlog of cases and some demonstrate incompetency through arbitrary judgement. Zambia's customs administration is influenced by corruption and bribery. Listed among the public institutions is the customs service, where bribes are frequently demanded by staff. Corruption is a challenge for foreign companies doing business within the Zambian natural resources sector. Reporting practices in the extractive industry are weak and often lack transparency, with a very limited amount of data on granted licenses and contracts disclosed to the public.[149]

L-R P.W Botha, F. W De Klark, Nelson Mandela, Thabo Mbeki and Jacob Zuma Schabir Shaik

Chiuba

Chapter 6

North Africa

Egypt was a British protectorate in 1915 but achieved full independence in 1922, becoming a kingdom under the rule of Muhammad Ali's dynasty, lasting until 1952. On 22–26 July 1952, a group of disaffected army officers (the "free officers") led by Muhammad Naguib and Gamal Abdel Nasser overthrew King Farouk, whom the military blamed for Egypt's poor performance in the 1948 war with Israel. Gamal Abdel Nasser established the Republic in Egypt and ended the monarchy rule in Egypt, following the 1952 Egyptian revolution. Egypt was ruled autocratically by three presidents over the following six decades, by Nasser from 1954 until his death in 1970, Anwar Sadat from 1971 until his assassination 1981, and by Hosni Mubarak from 1981 until his resignation in the face of the 2011 Egyptian Arab-Spring. A nation-wide survey conducted in mid-2009 by the Cairo-based Al-Ahram Centre for Political and Strategic Studies found that almost fifty percent of small and medium businesses in Egypt are forced to offer government clerks cash bribes in order to obtain business licenses and must continually bribe them in order to avoid fines. The report found the phenomenon so wide-spread that business-owners were not only forced to pay bribes for legal interests; even to obtain permits, they have no need, and neither the payers nor the recipients of bribes consider the transaction to be a bribe, but rather consider it to be normal payment for services rendered. In other words, it is part of the cost of doing business in Egypt.[150] Given the large number of cases reported to the Prosecutor-General's office in the aftermath of Egypt's 25 January 2011 revolution, the Administrative Control Authority office opened an investigation into thousands of reports against officials in the former regime for obtaining financial gain from corruption for themselves or others. A large number of those officials have been brought to stand criminal trial, notably the former Head of State, his two sons and many former ministers.

In the face of this, we must guard against witch hunt or settle scores. Because of the complex ties these persons had and the great power they wielded by virtue of their former prominent public functions, they were able to transfer vast sums of money gained from crimes of corruption out of the country, which impeded Egypt's development. 36.5 million dollars in financial instruments, properties in Madrid and Marbella, and luxury vehicles belonging to Hosni Mubarak, the former president of Egypt have been frozen. The Spanish investigation into the assets located in Spain belonging to the President Mubarak, his family, associates and related entities encompassed over 130 individuals. In May 2014, Mr. Mubarak was convicted on charge of embezzlement and sentenced to three years' imprisonment. But since has been acquitted. According to the May 11, 2011 statement by the Swiss Federal Department of Foreign Affairs, $428,373,000 US in assets held by Egyptian individuals belonging to the former Mubarak government had been frozen in Switzerland. The statement noted: The freezing of these assets does not demonstrate their legal or illegal origin. Thus, it is now up to the Egyptian judicial authorities to determine, through criminal proceedings, whether these assets were illicitly acquired. The Swiss Government announced that it had passed a special ordinance blocking any assets in Switzerland of the former President Mubarak and parties close to him.

L-R Gamal Nasir, Anwar Sadat and Hosni Mubarak

At independence in 1956, **Tunisia** was an efficient, virtuous civil service with a well-trained corps of technicians inherited from the French provincial period, stood ready to administer the new state and its modernization plans. In 1957, Tunisia became a republic, with Habib Bourguiba as the first President and the country's major reformist. He wasn't too keen to give up power but reports of senility ended his rule with a bloodless coup in 1987. Although he was hardly a democrat, Bourguiba's thirty years at the helm were free from the extravagant corruption of his successor, Zine al-Abidine Ben Ali, who was ousted in the revolution of January 2011.[151] Ben Ali ascended to the office of President on 7 November 1987, after doctors attending to the former president filed an official medical report declaring President Bourguiba medically debilitated and unable to fulfill the duties of the presidency. January 26, 2011 INTERPOL released a communique that Mr. Ben Ali's arrest was sought by Tunisia on charges of alleged property theft and illegal transfer of foreign currency. Ben Ali fled to Saudi Arabia to escape the long arm of Tunisian law. In April 2014, the Swiss Federal Prosecutor's Office announced that it would unfreeze $40 million US Ben Ali sequestered in Swiss banks: The decision is the result of good collaboration with the Tunisian authority. The Tunisian authorities were able to provide enough evidence to allow the monies, which were linked to Tunisia's former autocrat Zine el-Abidine Ben Ali, to be returned prematurely. It has been rumored that Ben Ali and his family got whatever they wanted when they want it, from yacht to land and other valuable properties. The World Bank determined that while the firms owned by Ben Ali and his families accounted for only three percent of economic output, they controlled twenty-one percent of net private sector profits. Familial corruption is certainly frustrating to many Tunisians, but beyond the rumors of money-grabbing is an irritation that the well-connected can live outside the law. One Tunisian lamented that Tunisia was no longer a police state, it had become a government run by the mafia. Corruption is a problem that is both political and economic. The lack of transparency and accountability that is characteristic of Tunisia's political system correspondingly afflicts the economy, damaging the investment climate and fueling a tradition of venality. There are still several examples of foreign companies or investors being pressured into joining with the "right" partner. The prime example remains McDonald's the global fast food chain, failed entry into Tunisia was because McDonald's chose to limit Tunisia to one franchisee not of the Government of Tunisia's choosing. The whole deal was scuttled by the Government Of Tunisia's refusal to grant the necessary authorization and McDonald's unwillingness to play the game by granting a license to a franchisee with Family connections. Corruption is the big gorilla in the room; it is the problem everyone knows about, but no one can publicly acknowledge [152] Ben Ali and his cronies tweaked the laws to serve the interests of his family and those close to him to the detriment of the rest of Tunisia.

Bin Ali

COL Gaddafi came to power by copying Gamal Nasser of Egypt overthrowing King Idris in a coup in 1969, ten years after independence, and Libya embarked on a radically new chapter in its history for forty-two years. Libyan leader Muammar Qaddafi, a dexterous Soldier, politician manipulated local rivals and his own sons so that he could remain in power and possibly pass the throne to one of his sons like what is obtainable in North Korea and Egypt. COL Gaddafi's power was absolute, exercised through "revolutionary committees" formed by regime loyalists. Libya was ranked 146 among 178 countries on the Corruption Perception Index in 2010. In 2006, Libyan residents ranked the police force highest in their perception of the spread of corruption in the country. This happens like in the other African countries by a traffic officer stopping drivers, seize their drivers' licenses or car-related documents; the return of the drivers' car document would take the form of trading the license for money, cigarettes, or even a sandwich.[153]

  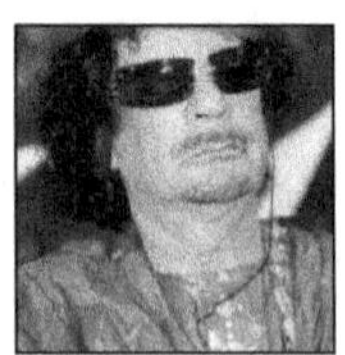 

Gaddafi as a young Captain and a state visit to Uganda with Idi Amin and son Saif Islam

Chapter 7

How the game is played

Most African nations have conceptual constitutions and institution but very few have them in truth; the formal rules of the constitution do not realistically direct the conduct of rulers and other political leaders in most places most of the time. In so far as rules are followed by African rulers, it is only after they have been changed by the ruler or oligarchy in question to suit his or their personal-political convenience. But rules of expediency are not, recognizably, rules of institutional government. They are better perceived as conduits of power and not as normative confinements on power, they are the symbols of political authoritarianism, which is closely allied to personal rule. In institutionalized systems, personal calculations are made, within the universally accepted rules and requirements of the political game; in personal terms, such calculations are not mediated by reference to rules agreed to by all leaders and factions, while the governing party and its rivals in a constitutional democracy will go to great lengths to win elections, they will not seek to abolish elections to stay in power or manipulate the electoral rules or their supervision to the point where they no longer are basically fair. By contrast, such manipulation is precisely what citizens see in African leadership authoritarian regime".[154]

Jackson and Rosenberg also insist that in a situation where personal rule triumphs over institutional government, African leaders take precedence over rules, they are not effectively bound by his office and able to change their authority and powers to suit personal or political needs. In the African system, the ruler and other leaders act as the judge and jury, take precedence over the formal rules of the civic contest; the rules do not effectively regulate political behavior or apply to them, and therefore cannot predict or anticipate conduct from knowledge of the rules. They are also the executioner. To put this in old-fashioned, comparative government terms, the State is a government of men and not of law.[155]

The common political intrigue associated with both the civilian and dictatorial military regime is the propensity of the political elites to hang on to power through electoral malpractices. Lately, an orchestrated manipulation of the constitutional rules in the impoverish land locked country in the southern region of Africa, Burundi and Rwanda in 2015 and in the West African country of Nigeria in 2007. In these countries, there is a constitutional mandate for the President to serve only two terms but the Presidents of these countries manipulated the constitution to allow them to continue for the third term. This has led tragically to the loss of lives in Burundi. Unfortunately, both the presidents of Burundi and Rwanda won the third term election contestation. In Burundi, this led to many tragic loses, including prominent and influential Burundians. Credit goes to Nigerian Parliament, which struck down such malfeasance during President Obasanjo's term.

Until 1973, twenty-one countries in Africa participated in a coup d'état and the number has risen since. However, discontent with the discreditable performance of the ruling politicians provides only a superficial explanation of the recurrent phenomenon of coups in the emergent states. When the onion is peeled back, deeper motivations are probed; most of the coups are product of the ambition for political power and financial greed among the different elements in the society elite.[156]

The leaders of some of these African countries lack legitimacy owing to the fact that some of them were former rebel leaders. Leaders such as President Yoweri Musevini of Uganda, Paul Kagame of Rowanda before they were properly elected as presidents, former President of Liberia Charles Taylor who is convicted of crimes against humanity serving prison sentence at the International Criminal Court, Hague, Switzerland . Some came to power by overthrowing a democratically elected government like President Omar Bashir of Sudan, COL Gaddafi of Libya, FL LT J. J. Rawlings in Ghana and some of them are in power for close to thirty years and upon their death, a close family member will assume power in such countries as Democratic Republic of Congo, Benin Republic, Gabon, Togo and Egypt. The leaders also exploited public opinion," by defusing inherent potential sources of opposition, suppressing and placating, employing reversal and insistence tactics in a bid to ensure a delicate balance of legitimacy". In some cases, brutal suppression of the opposition such as imprisonment and murder which happened in Guinea with the first Secretary General of Organization of African Unity and assassination of Patrice Lumumba in Congo. African leaders ensure an unstable political environment to facilitate self- perpetuation in power while corruption assume a new dimension, becoming a national virtue rather than vice. Power consolidation is through the manipulation of the fragile ethnic relationships made the overriding objectives of national development and interest a failed project while a few individuals emerge as power brokers and king makers.

African presidents are suffering from messianic hallucinations; who believe that without them, their countries cannot survive. This may be why Africans have dinosaurs as leaders. Leaders like Zimbabwe's Robert Mugabe, Angolan, Jose Eduardo dos Santos, Paul Biya of Cameroun and Uganda's Yowerei Museveni, who have presided over their countries, an average of thirty-three years apiece. But the simple example of Nelson Mandela, whose funeral many, if not all of them attended, despite his cult-like followership spent only one term in office, smashing the myth of presidential messiahs. This is why African leaders, who were quick to condemn the coup attempt in Burundi also, have the duty to call Nkurunziza to order. Why would a leader endanger the good health and wellbeing of his country by clinging to power? But I am not confident that they or the African Union (AU) would be willing or courageous enough to tell Nkurunziza and his likes the truth or speak truth to power because such ideas are very tempting at any particular time during their presidency.

Africa has been a caricature and the butt of jokes for the whole world not just because of corruption but corruption and bribery has compounded this quandary.

The majority of African Union (AU) members came together and adopted anti-corruption principles. This AU Convention on Preventing and Combating Corruption in Maputo, Mozambique in July 2003 was signed by all except eight members. What would be the good and compelling reason for any country to refuse the signatory of a corruption and bribery prevention principle, if not for discrete nefarious action and to defraud their individual countries? This is not a discussion on global climate change or global carbon reduction and sequestration issues but against government corruption in high places for the sake of good governance and national progress.

Africa was a pawn or a ragdoll in the fight between Capitalism and Communism that the most brutal of these dictators like Samuel Doe in Liberia were courted by President Reagan, willing to look the other way as long as communism is defeated. In Angola, where the former Soviet Union (USSR) with the help of Fidel Castro of Cuba supported the Civil war which lead to the death of a charismatic leader, Joseph Savimbi. Joseph Savimbi's U.S.-based supporters ultimately proved successful in influencing the Central Intelligence Agency (CIA) to route covert weapons and recruit guerrillas for Savimbi's war versus Angola's Marxist government, which greatly intensified and prolonged the conflict and the loss of many lives. This is a country where US nor USSR has any national interest or goal. This is similar to the war waged by US and USSR in the 1980's in Nicaragua with Daniel Ortega and the Sandinistas, in El-Salvador and Guatemala in South America.

The World Bank, admitting cultural variations, dismissed the notion that corruption was a Western concept. It is argued that in all associations, there is a peculiarity between gift-giving and corruption because it is transparent and not clandestine, the scale is modest as opposed to life changing, the benefits may or may not be shared by the community and there is no violation of public trust and rights. The same argument cannot be made of corruption. It can be brazenly done with an aura of transparency only benefiting the recipient, his family and friends.[157] This is similar to one micturating or urinating on one's self; it is a warm feeling experienced by the individual that quickly disappear. This loose interpretation of corruption is an attempt by the elite to obfuscate and use illegitimate exorbitant grafting as gift giving in an effort to sway the public official to making decisions that favor the gift giver.[158] In prosecuting such crimes, a majority consider that justice is unequal and that treatment rests on the social status of the person being prosecuted. If you are rich and connected, you are not prosecuted or the matter white washed. Children of lesser gods would have the proverbial "book thrown at them" for minor infraction. This is not only happening in Burkina Faso and Mauritania but all the way to Zimbabwe and every country in Africa. Judicial proceedings are very expensive and victims of corruption often prefer not to seek redress. This is because of the prohibitive cost and the length of time required in adjudicating such proceeding.

The enforcement or implementation of these anti-corruption laws where they exist remains problematic in the continent of Africa. The government officials should strongly consider implementing or enforcing these existing laws without fear or favor. The government's Financial Intelligence Unit should carry out prompt investigations of corruption allegations and impose stricter sanctions on individuals or companies found in violation of these legal instruments. Where the laws are unclear, enact a comprehensive Access to Information Law (Right to Information Law) this is similar to the Freedom of Information Act in USA. This law would ensure a proactive disclosure of information and promote transparency and accountability in procurement with respect to all government contracts. An access to information law ensures an active inclusion of citizens in the business of the government. This is achievable where there are secure and reliable information storage systems and a system of accountability and responsibility of the government to preserve documents particularly those relating to public expenditure. It is also evidentiary if a particular individual or entity is being prosecuted.

Mandating officials to divulge information about their wealth before entering and after exiting public service, allows a public employee's wealth to be monitored and thus deter the more determined or those tempted to purloin from the public but fearful their unethical doing might be revealed. Those wealthy enough to venture into public life must have their assets placed in blind trust, to avoid the appearance of impropriety. A confidential disclosure requires that the agency administering such disclosures must be politically neutral and enjoys the confidence of the citizens and public officials. However, this is a difficult condition to meet in a country like the Democratic Republic of Congo where no such laws exist. A public disclosure regimen will allow civil society and the media to help enforce the program and report to the citizens when such laws are violated. This disclosure system should of course be backed by strict sanctions in cases where employees lie about their assets, income, investments or level of indebtedness as in the case of the President of Nigeria's House of Representatives Mr. Saraki. Saraki operated three different accounts in three currency denominations. The first account, according to him, is a naira currency account; the second is a dollar account, while the third is a pound sterling account. Over N600,000 per deposit was made into his account fifty times a day, according to Nigerian financial crimes watchdog EFCC. Among Dr. Saraki's assets include under movable property, the following cars and the price in Nigerian Currency: Mercedes S320 valued at N16m, Mercedes S500 valued at N20m, Mercedes G500 value at N6m, MercedesV220 valued at N2m, Ferrari 456GT valued at N25m, Navigator valued at N15m,

Mercedes MN240 valued at N8.5m, Peugeot 406 valued at N2.9m, Mercedes CLK 320 valued at N9m, Mercedes E320 valued at N11m, Mercedes G500 bullet proof valued at N45m, Mercedes S500 valued at N30m, Lexus Jeep bullet proof valued at N30m, Lincoln Navigator bullet proof valued at N25m. Saraki has a definite proclivity towards high performance cars. He has enough to start a Mercedes dealership in his compound. It was recently reported that the government is dropping or amending the charges against Mr. Saraki.

The immunity from trial enjoyed by public official in Nigerian polity which shields them from prosecution until after their term limit. This is awkward because if successive party wins the election, the reluctance to investigate its predecessor is almost nonexistence. It becomes the "old boys club." When such financial irregularity is discovered, it may be decades. The perpetrators may be dead or no longer in public service. Where statute of limitation is in effect, it would have already expired.

It is not enough for anti-corruption efforts to stop at preventing corruption and imposing sanctions on those guilty of corrupt practices. The government should make efforts at asset recovery. The bank accounts of those found blameworthy of corruption should be frozen and efforts made at ensuring that assets that are the proceeds of corruption crimes are returned to the nation. Financial institutions should be obligated to scrutinize the deposits in high value accounts made by prominent public officials inside and outside of the country for the purpose of detecting and reporting to the appropriate authorities any suspicious transaction. If the transactions are legitimate, the public official has nothing to worry about. Public officials with interests in financial accounts in foreign countries should be obligated to report that relationship to appropriate authorities and maintain appropriate records related to those accounts. This is not to prevent these public officials from having foreign bank accounts but it is safeguarding their financial interests and make them accountable and responsible.

The current institutional mechanisms to fight corruption on the African continent, notably the courts and the Financial Intelligence Units are weak, given the fact that many individuals have been dismissed from their posts on charges of corruption, but very few have been prosecuted and sentenced by the courts. If the particular nation lacks the means to investigate these crimes, they must seek the competencies and investigative capacities of countries able and willing to assist.

Owing to the fact that the courts lack judicial independence makes a mockery of the efforts against corruption and the judicial system when everyone can be paid off or bought. At the center of anti-corruption fight, is the willingness of the political leadership at the highest level to confront corruption. This is a multi-stake holder initiative that integrates the public and private sectors as well as civil society, all of which will benefit from a more open, stable and predictable government.

Public participation in decision making is an essential element to any transparent, accountable and democratic political system. Civil non-profit organizations play an important role in such participatory mechanisms, providing a link between citizens and decision makers and uncovering corrupt practices. At a time when trust in government's commitment to fight corruption is at an all-time low and declining, it is imperative to allow civil societies to participate in efforts aimed at curbing corruption. If civil society is not on board, it will make it harder to hold the government officials to account and easier for corruption to continue flourishing.

It would be unfair to end this exposé without pointing out that corruption is a worldwide phenomenon and is not isolated to poor, politically unstable and struggling economies like the DRC, Somalia, Sudan, Syria, among others.[159] African electorates must begin to evaluate the credentials of people running for elected positions in their constituencies and end hero worship where drug kingpin win election or crowned paramount kings and local chiefs. Election of candidate(s) should be based on patriotism, accountability and moral transparency in order to curtail the culture of impunity and the danger of running into yet another round of chaos in the continent.[160]

Kagame is widely admired and respected on the continent, and considered a shoo-in for the presidency of the African Union if he ever wants the job. The gravest charges against Kagame's regime relate to the actions of his army and the atrocities committed during the civil unrest in Rwanda and possible political assassination of his former intelligence chief and opposition in South Africa. There is clear evidence that the Rwanda Patriotic Front committed systematic massacres of Hutus both in Rwanda when they assumed power, then in Congo. According to UN reports, the Rwandan military has also plundered some $100 million worth of gold, diamonds, tin, timber and other minerals from war-ravaged eastern Congo.[161] There has never been a shortage of autocrats in Africa, but very few of them have been so driven and determined to better their countries instead, and most have concentrated on enriching themselves and shoring up their power and political base with patronage. Kagame has shown Africa that strong leadership can turn a country around, and that a strong leader shows no quarter to corruption.[162] Currently, Kagame is considered a benevolent authoritarian. The strong hand needed to pull Rwanda forward into a better future, and not an incorrigible despot like General Sani Abacha of Nigeria or Yoweri Museveni of Uganda, Murmur Gaddafi etc. who wish to remain in power perpetually.

Although military coups and election violence are becoming rarer in Africa, election poll rigging and manipulation remain rife, shambling the continent's self-governing progress. "We have this paradox where the number of elections is increasing but the quality of these elections and those being elected are decreasing," said Nic Cheeseman, an associate professor of African studies at Oxford University.

It is the seriousness and commitment shown by the political leadership in the current Nigerian President General Buhari that will convince local indigenes and other foreign countries that it is not corrupt business as usual in Africa and assist towards recovering looted money stashed in nameless foreign bank accounts in Switzerland, England and the Cayman Island, and most recently, Panama after the release of the Fonseca Papers. Who knew that Panama is a heaven for Corrupt African Leaders, tax cheats and shadow Companies. Many of the leaders named in the Fonseca papers are probably shaking in their boots because they do not know when the other shoe will fall. Although the tactics employed in obtaining papers are not condoned but it is difficult to argue otherwise.

Chapter 8

Solution

Multitudes of African children do not have enough to eat and many are forced to shut their eyes every night, hungry with bloated empty stomach and visibly numbered ribs that ache with each breath. Illiteracy has gained a vice-like grip on Liberian children for example that their chances of competing in the global economy range from zero to negative. If life is a poison, Liberian children are drinking it by the bucket. The HIV/AIDS epidemic and other health malaises have beleaguered the continent that morbidity and mortality rates continue to soar even for preventable diseases. Preventable diseases that have low mortality rate are killing children and pregnant mothers at levels not seen anywhere else in the world. In such a climate, stalled by helplessness and hopelessness, one wonders how corrupt officials rest their head at night to sleep. Let it be noted that these same political figures will go to England, USA, Germany and India for medical treatment, and yet they cannot replicate such advances in their respective countries. Those ill equipped to afford the treatment are relegated to their country's nonexistent health care system for care are doomed to early death.

A clear link exists between corruption and the nature of governance in Africa, and this cannot be disputed. With the entire continent's public infrastructure in ruins and civil servants earning wages that are unable to sustain them and their families, thus promoting a fertile environment for corruption. The government neglect's its oversight responsibilities and pays lip service to the subject matter and the subject matter being corruption and bribery, poor social standards, insecurity, food shortage, poor education and its effect on their countries and future generations. [163]

On a continent where deception is excessive, inequality is high, it stands the test of logic that in a highly disproportion and corrupt society, everyone is equally deprived. If poor governance contributes to lower growth and harmful outcomes to the nation and continent, weak rudimentary economic conditions facilitate corruption across the entire spectrum of African community.[164]

The military is misguided with a serial coup plots as a means to leadership hierarchy. Armed forces takeover and coup d'état is always carried out on the pretext of bad governance and corruption but it is very strange that military regimes too become victim of corruption and eventually collapse. Military establishment interventions are always followed by the announcement that it is for a very short duration but ultimately, military officers fall in love with power and absolute power corrupts for example Sani Abacha of Nigeria and Yoweri Museveni of Uganda.[165] In Africa, Kenya and Tanzania have been spared from this scourge but not the corruption. Education remains a better fortification to freedom, independence and economic emancipation than a corrupt military regime or corrupt civilian government. Structural reorganization of the armed forces, re-training and re-orientation of its men and women in the armed forces must be instituted if the armed forces of African nations are ever fit for its purpose, which is the defense of the territorial integrity of their nations and not to control, intimidate, imprison and sometimes kill those who morally disagree with the current governing philosophy.

Immunity from prosecution while in office boldly inserted in the constitution, are the type of incentive that can be easily and are often abused if they find their way into the open hands of a political miscreant.[166] Such are constitutions not seen in developed countries. President Clinton was impeached for lying to the congress of US and President Nixon resigned from office than face prosecution by the US congress. The reasoning behind this is after all that corrupt officials and their crimes will be forgotten by the time the incumbent leaves office. Better yet, if the replacement is from one's own political party then the chances of any investigation, prosecution or punishment will greatly diminish.

There must be simple, strict and clear asset declaration procedures for politicians, senior civil servants, and police and Judicial Service officials, including judges. For avoidance of doubt, those who have life tenure must declare their assets at regular intervals after their appointment. The asset declaration process must be strengthened by publication of declared assets, and introduction of the necessary powers for the Serious Financial Fraud Office, on clearly documented suspicion, to investigate covered officials living above their means. This may be corruption or treason which is peddling of state secret in exchange for money or protection. This means that if a District Chief Executive builds two mansions within four years of coming into Office, can be a basis for the investigation of the official's assets. This worked in Singapore and it can work in Ghana, Nigeria, Kenya, Uganda, Liberia, Sierra Leone etc. The remedy to this level of corrupt gift giving and receiving is to limit the value of the gift to twenty dollars. Any gift greater than this becomes a ward of the country and declared as such. If the recipient want's this gift by all means, he then, can pay a fair market value for the gift.

In 2013, 22,000 public officials in South Africa were charged with misconduct for corrupt activities compares to Brazil, twenty-five people were convicted of using public funds to buy political support. Among those convicted was the former president's Chief of Staff, the second most powerful man in the country.[167]

Countries in Africa must strengthen the people and institutions charged with fighting corruption. Restructuring of the Police force and removal of the police from direct control by political authorities may reduce extra judicial killings, intimidation and detention of political opponents. These reforms must end the incestuous relationship between the Police, Criminals and Politicians that fuel corruption and undermine accountability and the rule of law. Implementation of the Freedom of Information bill, so that citizens can demand information from their government for financial and political activities. It will also lend transparency to public governance of the countries that make up the African Union. Africa and Africans have fought corruption through the force of ambiguous dispositions long enough. Africa, now, must move towards institutional measures that have worked in other places and stop following the false messiahs of accountability by the various presidents of African countries of "I am the only one able to fix all your problems" while illegally bankrupting their country.[168]

The rise in drug trafficking and money laundering in recent times is not unrelated to the rise in corruption, poverty and get rich quick scheme in high places by ordinary citizens. This situation has not inspired good governance, which is negatively reflecting on the nations and continent's economic growth. The development of Zambia's business environment is hindered by corruption and a weak institutional framework. Companies encounter red tape and rampant bribery in all business operations, including registering a company, obtaining a construction permit, setting up utilities, and paying taxes. As a result of the inefficient and corrupt judicial system, foreign investors' property rights are not accurately protected or enforced thus forcing these businesses to move their services else- where. In addition, international trade is impeded by pervasive corruption and crime in Customs this situation is not helped by epileptic transmission of electricity. Companies regularly pay kickbacks and bribes in the tendering process for government contracts. [169] It is a recognized fact that good governance promotes economic growth, which in turn improves good governance thus, improving lives and social standard of its citizens. Stated differently, political corruption is negatively or inversely proportional to good governance. Thus, corruption and other aspects of poor governance and weak institutions, substantially hinder economic growth making multinational companies hesitant in investing in the continent of Africa with its largely untapped and mis-managed human capital and mineral resources. The misconception that poverty is the sole problem of Africans is misguided. The problem afflicting Africans is poor management and deprived administrative oversight. If those who manage the political welfare of the African countries are morally bankrupt, this parsimoniously bankrupts the nations and deprives its citizens. It is not just an eccentricity that no federal minister has resigned for dishonesty. It is almost impossible for an African Head of State to resign for the same. Instead, they will fraudulently win more elections to remain in power. Corruption impair everyone, if people are hopeless they turn to violence because the outcome is inconsequential to them. Consider the rise of religious extremism; Africa is ripe for such violence and corruption. It is also ready to export it. For example, Al Shabaab in Somalia and its affect in Kenya and the surrounding countries.

Chapter 9

Grand corruption is a threat to the national security of any nation especially African nations. And nowhere in the world is the link between corruption and national insecurity greater than in Africa. This is because the huge numbers of dis-enfranchised population create a breeding ground for political, tribal, religious extremism and extremist ideology. In Nigeria, the sophistication of crimes committed by the youths range from Cyber /internet crimes called 419, cultism, murder for hire, cheating and stealing. They are now formed into small armies of kidnappers and oil bunkereres.[170] The leadership of African nations has stolen their nations into physical and financial insecurity. Soldiers are, disillusioned, yet asked to make the supreme sacrifice. Morale is obviously low that soldiers are reluctant to fight, flee and the resultant lawlessness is a complicated and seemingly intractable conflict with Boko Haram, Al Shabab, M23, Islamic Maghreb, LORD etc. due to the above factors, it seems attractive for young men and women to join these extremist organizations because they consider it a stepping stone to greater things after all, Muserveni, Charles Taylor, Kagame etc. were all presidents and one-time rebel leaders.

It has emerged in Nigeria that 2.1 billion dollars ear marked for the procurement of modern arms and ammunition to fight Boko Haram were parceled out to political cronies of former President Johnathan for illegal electoral manipulation by his embattled National Security Adviser COL Sambo. In societies where people link their collective poverty to the corruption and greed of the power elite, the fight against corruption cannot be the fight of one person but a kibbutz type cooperative effort of all Africans irrespective of the country because the problem transcends individual nation's boundaries.

Many of the African leaders claim that their country is democratic because they won the election, be it under questionable conditions and the presidents and prime ministers act as benevolent messiah, dictator and totalitarians. Dissent is a hallmark of representative democracy. It is invariably the first casualty in a move to establish a totalitarian government.[171] Many have been in power greater than twenty years and some prefers to die in office or be killed for them to relinquish power. The following African leaders compete on who will be in power the longest. Ben Ali of Tunisia, twenty-three years as the president until he was forced into exile.

Hosni Mubarak of Egypt, with thirty years in power, was unceremoniously removed from office during the Arab spring. His life sentence was over turned in 2015. He is now being pushed around in a hospital bed, not a wheel chair.

Teodoro Obiang Nguema of Equetorial Guinea (thirty-two years), Jose Santos Angola (thirty-two years), Robert Mugabe, Zimbabwe (thirty-one years) senile and frail still in power and probably will until death.

Paul Biya of Cameroon (twenty-nine years), Yoweri Musaveni of Uganda (twenty-seven years).

Since there are no term limits, he will remain in power until self- imposed term limit, death or uprising removes him from office. Recently, Omar Bashir of Sudan stated that he will leave office in 2020. This is after over thirty years in power. In his fickle mind, he thinks he is doing Sudan a favor. Blaise Campore of Burkina Faso was just deposed by military coup September 2015, he popped smoke and went into self- imposed exile in Ivory Coast. Murmar Qadaffi (forty-two years) escaped to a drainage ditch outside of Tripoli during the civil -war, he was later captured under a drainage ditch and murdered. No one extended a life line to him. His son Saif al-Islam is on trial in Libya. You do not have to be a rocket scientist to be certain how this will end. It is just a matter of time. These are reckless, incorrigible despots with skewed perception of reality.

Chapter 10

The African continent is fractured along tribal, religious, ethnic lines, any devolution from such amalgamation will create a mass exodus to areas where one faction based on tribe or religion predominates and afford greater sense of security example Biafran region during the Nigeria civil war, Rwanda, Hutus and Tutsis, and the Central African Republic between the Selekas and the Barakas. In the Balkans which was divided into three parts Croats, Serbs and the Muslims in Bosnia. This will lead to more instability, especially if the region is mineral rich. Tribal cleansing will be perpetrated against the weaker tribe instead of amalgamation and harmony. African must work harder to escape ethnic and tribal bigotry, which is comparatively crippling the countries from Burundi to Zimbabwe and from Accra to Timbuktu and all the countries in between.

The policies and actions of African nations should greatly influence the continent's peace, prosperity and security. China is flexing its financial and military might in the whole of Africa, building substandard infrastructure, railroads in Nigeria which was severely modified during President Yar Adua's brief regime, Ethiopia, power generation plant and supplying jet fighters to Sudan the prosecution of the Darfurians of Central Sudan. The countries of Africa must have the will and project that will through electoral governance by making it clear and unambiguous to its leaders that kleptocracy, insecurity, poor education and substandard, infrastructure will not be tolerated. In this quest, many may die and it will be the premium paid for corrupt free society like the civil right protests, the death is the price in human currency paid for corrupt free society or the Arab Spring in Egypt, Morocco, Algeria. The Continuing violence in the North-East of Nigeria by Boko Haram—in the south by Movement for the Emancipation of Niger Delta (MEND) organization, Lord's Resistance Army in the Central of Africa, al-Shabaab in Somalia, and Kenya, Islamic Maghreb in North Africa, the Tuaregs in Mali and M23 Rebels in Congo basin—is exacting a considerable toll on the lives, livelihood and progress of Africans that live in these areas. Individually and collectively, these terrorists' activities could further destabilize the continent, which will increase the hardship on an already impoverished and financially stressed continent. The terrorist organizations tolerate some cooperation amongst themselves in the exchange of hostages, arms, ammunition, target acquisition and sharing of intelligence. By such action, African nations may not live in peace with itself or with its neighbors. In conflicts where militant groups are deeply involved, war became a ultimate political power because they want to take the helms of the country rather than an extension of political power. Over time, a growing number of stakeholders emerge who become dependent on criminal economy generated by the ongoing conflict similar to what happened in Liberia with Charles Taylor and Fouday Sanko in Sierra Leone. Illegal diamond trade became the source of revenue to finance the illegal war and enrich the individual war lords. Some politicians and security agents of neighboring states have been known to benefit from such illicit actions. And some governments have relied on such criminal actions to meet other national security interests.[172]

It must be said that criminal networks are both fueling corruption and threatening Africa's precious wildlife, and with it, the tourism that many African countries count on to generate foreign reserve. In other words, wild life tourism is the only export commodity these nations own for example Uganda, Kenya, Tanzania. America and the responsible world also stand with Africans in the fight against wildlife trafficking and poaching so that these precious wild animals remain in the wild forests and open grassland of the African plain, its natural habitat not China, Japan, USA or Great Britain for generations. Big game hunting should only be done in private reservations. Care must be taken to protect the big games that migrate from public to private reservations.

Strengthening the central government authorities should be encouraged to alleviate the question of revenue sharing and allocation in countries that are rich in natural resources such as gold, crude oil, diamond, iron ore etc. and this is the entire African continent. The political will must be there to fight corruption. The former president of Peru, Alberto Fujimori was convicted for various crimes, absconded to Japan, his ancestral home but was extradited back to Peru and he is serving a life sentence in prison. These crooks can run but they cannot hide. The long arm of the law will fetch them out but it is dependent on the willingness of the ruling elite in the individual countries to enforce the existing laws and ensure that these crooks are properly prosecuted.

Bribery requires one to give and another to accept either may initiate this corrupt exercise and many are not shy of asking. In Africa, the culture of corruption extends into every aspect of public life making it extremely difficult to eradicate. Some African leaders are well intentioned, once in power, those determination and intentions fizzle because they know that their regime will surely end and any investigation carried out by other administration during their time will be re-visited on them after they are gone from office. It is a sort of ersatz gentleman's agreement. "I will not investigate my predecessor and my successor will not investigate me." Theodor Roosevelt said that to destroy this invisible government, is to dissolve the unholy alliance between corrupt business and corrupt politics, is the first task of the statesmanship. The legal framework for fighting bribery and corruption in all African countries is government show of good will in strengthening the law already passed by the Legislature; but, anti-corruption laws lack sufficient oversight. President Mwanawasa demonstrated his stance against corruption by removing his minister of Land for improper conduct. When there is visibility from the top, it re-enforces the belief to ordinary citizens that the fight to eradicate corruption is being effective and not just a duplicity or double standard. According to Obasanjo, the former president of Nigeria said African leaders were failing their people because they had not been able to prevent marginalization in their societies, prevent injustice, reduce unemployment, reduce poverty and they had not embraced democracy and good governance.

The lack of progress in the obliteration of corruption in Africa is due to absence of clear and unambiguous political will. African leaders cannot proclaim anti-corruption measure for everyone else but remain engaged in looting the country's treasury. Legal weakness and poor enforcement of the anti-corruption reforms are impediment to proper law and order in the continent of Africa.[173] Insufficient implementation of anti-corruption legislation coupled with impunity among public officials lead to very high corruption risks across all sectors of African community. African citizens should not accept that corruption is a topic downgraded to hushed voices with quick fleeting look over the shoulder to see who may be watching in complete condescension of the law. Stiffer penalties need to be imposed on public officials convicted of corruption. This will send a clearer message to the remaining officials, thus deterring some from engaging in such corrupt activities. But there are some brazen thieves who will stop at nothing to improperly enrich themselves at the cost of the public.

Irrevocably, there is a need for increased protection for whistle blowers within local, state, federal government institutions and the public sector in general. This erstwhile will ensure safety of those who report cases of corruption, also encourage others to do the same. In the United States, it is called whistle blower protection. The whistle blower will not lose their job or seniority in their place of employment. If any money is collected, the whistle blower is entitled to five to ten percent of such fund.

Only African leaders can end corruption in their countries. As African governments commit to taking action, the United States, Germany, Britain and the rest of the free world will work with individual African country to combat illicit financing, and promote good governance, transparency and strengthen the rule of law. Africa already has strong laws in place that say to U.S, German, Chinese, Israeli, Italian, British companies, you can't engage in bribery in other to do business.

Africa must overcome the greed that corrupt practices breed and move their countries into the part of success for all of its citizens and future generations.

Chapter 11

Progress

Pluto said that the penalty good men pay for indifference to public life is to be ruled by evil men.

There are notable changes in Kenya, Nigeria and many African countries. The Kleptocratic ministers and government authorities, at least in Nigeria, are returning part of the money stolen from Nigeria because General Buhari is bent on prosecuting them to avoid such fate; some are voluntarily retuning the looted funds. The grandson of Jomo Kenyatta, Uhuru Kenyatta in Kenya is sacking crooked ministers and replacing them with moderate officials. It should be noted that Uhuru Kenyatta was once indicted for atrocities committed against the Kenyan people during this first bid for the presidency by the International Criminal Court but the charges were later dismissed.

In an open letter to Nigerian National Assembly, Olusegun Obasanjo, the former President of Nigeria, said, "The purpose of election into the Legislative Assembly particularly at the national level is to give service to the nation and not for the personal service and interest of members at the expense of the nation which seemed to have been the mentality, psychology, mindset and practice within the National Assembly since the beginning of this present democratic dispensation. Where is patriotism? Where is commitment? Where is service? Governance without transparency will be a mockery of democracy ."[174] Although the former President of Nigeria was confronting the legislators in Nigeria, he might as well be deliberating with every elected official in the continent of Africa.

African leaders, call for citizenry to forfeit some gains to improve their society while the same African leaders live in explicit opulence. Swindlers, degenerates and opportunists who came to be very wealthy by corruption have suddenly become African leaders without genuine foundation, qualification, commitment or adequate preparation. Wealth, influence and patronage have permeated the system and generated pitiable reprobates who now masquerade as leaders. The famous Nigerian writer, Chinua Achebe said that the truest test of integrity is its blunt refusal to be compromised. In the end, Corruption weakens democracy, causes major failure in development, subverts formal process, makes economic planning difficult, stifles the implementation of public services projects and ruins a country.[175] Crude oil is being discovered in almost all the counties in Africa making the oil market less lucrative. USA and Germany are moving away from fossil fuel into self-sufficiency in energy consumption and generation, driving the price per barrel of oil lower than what it cost to produce. With this outlook and diversification in renewable energy, China, USA and the rest of the world may very well tell the African countries and its leaders to consume their oil, swim in it or worse yet push it into areas where the sun don't shine. This is the fate of African countries with monolithic economy that is dependent on oil.

It is painfully obvious that corruption stifles development. It drains off meager resources that could titivate infrastructure, strengthen education and public health systems. Corruption stacks the deck so high that entrepreneurs cannot get their ideas off the ground. Corruption erodes the state from inside out, sicken the justice system until there is no justice to be found, such as in Ghana and Nigeria, poisoning the police force until their presence becomes a source of insecurity rather than comfort. But this is not indigenous to Ghana; it is in every country in Africa. Corruption makes it impossible to respond effectively to crisis. It does not engender confidence in the citizens. The HIV/AIDS ravaging South Africa, pandemic Ebola Disease in Liberia, Sierra Leone, Guinea or Malaria in Nigeria or crippling drought in sub Saharan countries and out of this human crisis, someone is illegally profiting. This is illustrated by the saga in Nigeria where the former National Security Adviser, COL Sambo, under President Jonathan, illegally appropriated 2.1 billion dollars meant to procure arms and ammunition to fight the Boko Haram insurgency for electoral irregularities in Mauritania, Tunisia and Uganda where funds for childhood vaccination were misappropriated into the back pockets of politicians.[176]

Who is watching the watch man? Those appointed to watch the watchman are in cohort with the watchman. The citizens are seeing what the watchman is doing yet powerless, knowing who appointed the watchman. Consider, Nigeria's Chief of Defense Staff, Air Marshal Alex Badeh (rtd) (a position similar to the US Air Force, Chiefs of Staff) siphoned off over N3.9 billion, meant for the payment of salaries of Nigerian Air Force officials from the accounts of the Nigerian Air Force within one year, for his personal use. This is a malfunction of the Air Marshall for not returning the unspent fund back to the Nigerian national treasury. Air Marshal Alex Badeh devised a way out of his position and authorities to keep the excess fund. Someone in Ministry of Defense authorized this payment. Former Director of Finance and Accounts at the Nigerian Air Force, NAF, Air Commodore Salisu Abdullahi Yushau, rtd, told the Federal High Court in Abuja that the Chief of Defense Staff, Air Chief Marshal Alex Badeh, had a particular officer whose duty it was to monthly convert the sum of N558.2 million to dollars and dutifully bring the money to his official residence in Abuja, Nigeria. This officer is equally culpable, given that he is an accessory to the crime, since he facilitated the payment, knowing that it was wrong and did not inform proper authority to report the crime. As an officer in the Nigerian Air Force and a matter of code of conduct, it is illegal for an officer to comply with an illegal order. This is punishable under the Unified Code of Military Justice.

"Nothing will unlock Africa's economic potential more than ending the cancer of corruption. And you are right that it is not just a problem of Africa, it is a problem of those who do business with Africa as well. It is not unique to Africa, corruption exists all over the world, including in the United States. But here in Africa, corruption drains billions of dollars from economies that can't afford to lose hundreds no to mention of billions of dollars. This is money that could be used to create jobs and build hospitals, roads and schools. And when someone has to pay a bribe just to start a business or go to school, or get an official to do the job they're supposed to be doing anyway — that's not 'the African way.' It undermines the dignity of the people you represent," said Obama Barak

The African Union members did not need President Obama to tell them that corruption has no place in Africa. These African leaders may naively think that the foreign leaders do not know about their illegal sequestration of wealth in their nations. Africa is on the verge of greatness and it will require the assistance of all freedom loving nations of the world to help it get there. The Aids given to Africa must be tied to verifiable project with an oversight of the donor country or the money donated will go into the back pocket of the reigning leader. This population of disenfranchised, educated citizens of Africa are willing to earn a living doing respectable, dignified and legitimate work.

As China and India declines, Africa will rise because it has the excess human capital and natural resources. If the African nations can stem the drain of intellectuals leaving the continent for greener pastures elsewhere and pay close to the wage, these professional will get in an open market and they will remain in their countries. There is no institution of higher learning or hospital in England or USA that does not have highly trained Africans. It has been said that if you remove the Nigerian and Ghanaian doctors from some US hospitals, some will cease to function.

Africa is also a powder keg due to the same reasons. This tinder box is already burning in North Eastern Nigeria, Chad and Cameroon with Boko Haram, Al Shabaab in Somalia, Kenya, Central African Republic with the Seleka and the Baraka movement, Congo, Uganda with The Lord's Resistance Army and M23 militias, if the world turns a blind eye at the corruption in Africa, Africa will descend into chaos and threaten the religious, ethnic and tribal pluralism that make-up the fabric of African Quilt. This violence can also be exported to other nations inside and outside of Africa.

Africa and particularly the African leaders must remain blind to tribal, ethnicity, religious bigotry and eschew corruption when issues of Africa and its communities' development are concerned, otherwise Africa will never progress. If African leaders lack the differentiation and embark on tribal or ethnic nation building rather than country and nation building. Such practices obstruct unity, confidence, fairness, growth and progress of the nation. This is not an advocate for Pan Africanism because the magnitude and direction of globalization will force isolationism to fail. The whole world will continue to marginalize the richest continent in the world. The hope and future of Africa is in the collective destiny and progress of its people and the reawakened consciousness that corruption is a gift that benefits no one. In the end, African leaders must see themselves as African and not apart from Africa because all their parts are intertwined. Africa needs a true transformational leadership. A leadership of opportunities and not a leadership to escape from difficult situation and swindle the country of her public finance. A leadership of clarity and order not of perplexity, ambivalence, disorientation or puzzlement. A leadership of possibilities to move Africa forward economically, politically, socially progressive continent, devoid of corrupt practices, irregularity and incompetence. Corrupt actions of the African leaders have contributed to chaos and violence on the continent there-by alienating majority of the African citizen. The African leaders have failed to secure their individual countries, and thus economic development lags behind.

Governance in Africa should be on what you know and not who you know and where you come from, your pedigree should be less important and less significant than whom you are. The responsibilities remain Africans. The new crop of African leaders will face a monumental challenge of picking up the pieces of broken policies and misplaced priorities of past leadership. A truly publicly ardent person as Obafemi Awolowo stated that one should accept public office not for what he can get for himself such as the profit and glamour of office but for the possibility which it advances him of providing his people to the best of his talent, by advocating for their prosperity, security and the pursuit of happiness. These are the basic rights of a free and prosperous society as it is espoused in the United States Constitution. If this is good for the United States of America, it should also be good for every country in the African continent.

---

[1] Ricky Munyaradzi Mukonza, Anti-corruption and Local Governance in Zimbabwe January 2013, Vol. 10, No. 1, 39-48

[2] Amara M. Konneh Minister of Planning & Economic Affairs Economic Crimes, Corruption and the Conflict in Liberia: Policy Options for an Emerging Democracy and sustainable Peace The Perspective Atlanta, Georgia February 24, 2009

[3] Ekanpou Enewarideke still-on-sunset-and-a-coronation.vanguardngr.2016/02

[4] MAJ. GEN. Savre Kent

[5] Sun Nigerian Newspaper 14 July 2016

[6] Ekanpou Enewarideke still-on-sunset-and-a-coronation.vanguardngr.2016/02

[7] George Morara Corruption, a normal way of life in Kenya February 4, 2014

[8] Awolowo Letter from Prison to MAJOR GEN JTU Aguiyi Ironsi

[9] Michael M. Ogbeidi Political Leadership and Corruption in Nigeria Since 1960: A Socio-economic Analysis Associate Professor Department of History and Strategic Studies, University of Lagos, Nigeria

[10] ibid

[11] David Imhonopi Moses Urim Ugochukwu LEADERSHIP CRISIS AND CORRUPTION IN THE NIGERIAN PUBLIC SECTOR: AN ALBATROSS OF NATIONAL DEVELOPMENT Covenant University

[12] Obasanjo Olusegun: My Watch Now and then

[13] Michael M. Ogbeidi Political Leadership and Corruption in Nigeria Since 1960: A Socio-economic Analysis Associate Professor Department of History and Strategic Studies, University of Lagos, Nigeria

[14] David Imhonopi Moses Urim Ugochukwu LEADERSHIP CRISIS AND CORRUPTION IN THE NIGERIAN PUBLIC SECTOR: AN ALBATROSS OF NATIONAL DEVELOPMENT Covenant University

[15] Michael M. Ogbeidi Political Leadership and Corruption in Nigeria Since 1960: A Socio-economism Analysis Associate Professor Department of History and Strategic Studies, University of Lagos, Nigeria

[16] Obasanjo Olusegun:My Watch: Now and Then p. 402

[17] Michael M. Ogbeidi Political Leadership and Corruption in Nigeria Since 1960: A Socio-economicm Analysis Associate Professor Department of History and Strategic Studies, University of Lagos, Nigeria

[18] David Imhonopi Moses Urim Ugochukwu LEADERSHIP CRISIS AND CORRUPTION IN THE NIGERIAN PUBLIC SECTOR: AN ALBATROSS OF NATIONAL DEVELOPMENT Covenant University

[19] Reuters, December 17, 2004

[20] Obasanjo Olusegun My Watch: Now and Then p. 35

[21] NOAH EBIJE, sun 22 Jun 2015

[22] Obasanjo Olusegun. My Watch : Now and Then p.37

[23] ibid p222

[24] ibid p.37

[25] Kennedy Prince Modugu et al Forensic Accounting and Financial Fraud in Nigeria: An Empirical Approach, Department of Accounting Faculty of Management Sciences University of Benin, Nigeria

[26] Chibuike Ugochukwu Uche, (2001) "Nigeria: Bank Fraud", Journal of Financial Crime, Vol. 8 Iss: 3, pp.265 - 275

[27] Emperoh, And here are the looters of Failed Nigerian banks. 2:45pm On Jul 08, 2009

[28] ibid

[29] Kennedy Prince Modugu et al Forensic Accounting and Financial Fraud in Nige-

ria: An Empirical Approach, Department of Accounting Faculty of Management Sciences University of Benin, Nigeria

[30] Chibuike Ugochukwu Uche, (2001) "Nigeria: Bank Fraud", Journal of Financial Crime, Vol. 8 Iss: 3, pp.265 – 275

[31] O. A. Ogunlana, CORRUPTION: THE DIMENSIONS AND IMPLICATIONS FOR DEVELOPMENT IN NIGERIA

[32] Samuel OyadongaObasanjo very cunning, Tinubu very clever – Alamieyeseigha –Vangaurd Nigeria July 29 2015

[33] Obasanjo Olusegun: My Watch : Now and then p. 16

[34] Mike Ebonugwo & Bose Adelaja How military under-developed the Police Vangaurd Newspapers Nigeria November 23, 2015

[35] The many lies they said about Abacha- Al-Mustapha, Ben Agande, Vangaurd Nigeria. Read more at: http://www.vanguardngr.com/2016/05/many-lies-said-abacha/

[36] Obasanjo Olusegun: My Watch Now and Then p. 404

[37] Ibid p223

[38] O. A. Ogunlana, CORRUPTION: THE DIMENSIONS AND IMPLICATIONS FOR DEVELOPMENT IN NIGERIA

[39] Soni Daniel, Regional Editor, North & Levinus Nwagbuhiogu, Corruption NDDC Spends 1.3billion on Christmass Parties Vangaurd Nigeria

[40] O. A. Ogunlana, CORRUPTION: THE DIMENSIONS AND IMPLICATIONS FOR DEVELOPMENT IN NIGERIA

[41] Nigeria: Corruption and Misuse Rob Nigerians of Rights, January 31, 2007

[42] Omololu Fagbadebo Corruption, Governance and Political Instability in Nigeria Department of Political Science,Obafemi Awolowo University,Ile-Ife, Nigeria

[43] Michael M. Ogbeidi Political Leadership and Corruption in Nigeria Since 1960: A Socio-economic Analysis Associate Professor Department of History and Strategic Studies, University of Lagos, Nigeria

[44] Obasanjo Olusegun: My watch: Now and Thenp228

[45] By Dauda Garuba, Revenue Watch Nigeria Program Coordinator NIGERIA: Halliburton, Bribes and the Deceit of "Zero-Tolerance" for Corruption 9 April 2009

[46] Michael M. Ogbeidi Political Leadership and Corruption in Nigeria Since 1960: A Socio-economic Analysis Associate Professor Department of History and Strategic Studies, University of Lagos, Nigeri

[47] Omololu Fagbadebo Corruption, Governance and Political Instability in Nigeria

Department of Political Science, Obafemi Awolowo University, Ile-Ife, Nigeria

[48] Dauda Garuba, Revenue Watch Nigeria Program Coordinator NIGERIA: Halliburton, Bribes and the Deceit of "Zero-Tolerance" for Corruption 9 April 2009

[49] Michael M. Ogbeidi Political Leadership and Corruption in Nigeria Since 1960: A Socio-economic Analysis Associate Professor Department of History and Strategic Studies, University of Lagos, Nigeria

[50] ibid

[51] ibid

[52] David Imhonopi Moses Urim Ugochukwu LEADERSHIP CRISIS AND CORRUPTION IN THE NIGERIAN PUBLIC SECTOR: AN ALBATROSS OF NATIONAL DEVELOPMENT Covenant Universit[y]

[53] Omololu Fagbadebo Corruption, Governance and Political Instability in Nigeria Department of Political Science, Obafemi Awolowo University, Ile-Ife, Nigeria

[54] Nigeria: Corruption and Misuse Rob Nigerians of Rights, January 31, 2007

[55] Sun Newspaper, Chinelo Obongo and Job Osazuwa: We're Corrupt_Jibril 1 Aug 2016

[56] CORRUPTION: THE DIMENSIONS AND IMPLICATIONS FOR DEVELOPMENT IN NIGERIA

[57] Omololu Fagbadebo Corruption, Governance and Political Instability in Nigeria Department of Political Science, Obafemi Awolowo University, Ile-Ife, Nigeria

[58] ibid

[59] Vanguard Nigeria, July 19 2015

[60] Obasanjo Olusegun: My Watch: Now and Then

[61] ibid p220-221

[62] Christian Science Monitor tiny Togo- Opposition Leader Survives hit squad: Chris Stein 24 July 2013

[63] The Columbia Electronic Encyclopedia, 6th ed. Copyright © 2012, Columbia University Press. All rights reserved.

[64] US Department of State 2012 Investiment Climate Statement June 1012

[65] The Editors of Encyclopædia Britannica

[66] A Commentary- By The Liberian Democratic Future Posted September 28, 1998

[67] Stolen assets recovery initiate.: Charles taylor

[68] Dominic Harris The Independence 27 August 201

[69] Emmanuel Dolo, Ph. D. & Winsley Nanka, CPA Tracking the Tentacles of Corruption: The Case of Liberia's Atlanta, Georgia July 17, 200

[70] Sam K. Zinnah Sunday, January 24, 2010 The risk of impunity and Corruption in Liberia

[71] Wikipedia Liberia corruption.

[72] SIERRA LEONE: From Athens to an Ill-Run Sparta Monday, Jul. 28, 1980

[73] Foday Sankoh Sierra Leone's Rebel with a Cause by David Johnson

[74] David Tam-Baryoh Corruption in Sierra Leone Who Will Guard the Guards? Freetown, Sierra LeoneJanuary 15, 2002

[75] Alpha Kawusu Political corruption and economics in Sierra Leone 3 January 2012

[76] Diana Cammack□The Logic of African Neopatrimonialism: What Role for Donors?

[77] Alpha Kawusu Political corruption and economics in Sierra Leone 3 January 2012

[78] Alpha Kawusu, Political corruption and economics in Sierra Leone the Sierra Leone Telegraph 3 January 2012

[79] Kofi Akosah-Sarpong, The Corruption of Jerry Rawlings, | 16 September 2008

[80] ibid

[81] Hayford Atta-Krufi, The litany of Rawlings' corruption, 31 March 2014

[82] Arthur Kobina Kennedy - Ghanaian Chronicle 30 September 2009

[83] Tweneboah-Koduah, Nana Akua Corruption In Ghana, 14 March 2014

[84] GUINEA: Reputation for corruption worsens Irin News

[85] Ian Cobin and agencies, Beny Steinmets assoiate jailed over African investigation obstruction.,The Guardian 25 July 2014

[86] David Lewis, Insight: Surge in cocaine trade undermines Conde's bid to revive Guinea, Reuters Jan. 31 2014

[87] ibid

[88] ibid

[89] US Department of State 2014 Investment Climate Statement Bureau of Economic and Business Affairs June 2014

[90] The Editors of Encyclopædia Britannica Yoweri Kaguta Museveni President of Uganda Written

[91] Wikipedia Milton Obote

[92] Stolen Assets Recovery Initiative: Uganda 1996

[93] Johnson, Anne Museveni, Yoweri 1944(?)– Contemporary Black Biography 1993

[94] James Butty: Main opposition Leader Accuses Ugandan Police of Brutality; Oct 23 2016

---

[95] ibid

[96] ibid

[97] Marie Chene transparency International 4 March 2009

[98] ibid

[99] ibid

[100] ibid

[101] ibid

[102] ibid

[103] ibid

[104] ibid

[105] Marie Chene transparency International 4 March 2009

[106] The Economist, corruption in Kenya, How to ruin a country

[107] Mark Anderson: John Githongo: corruption in Kenya is poisoning politics

[108] Michela Wrong Everyone Is Corrupt in Kenya, Even Grandmothers' Is East Africa's economic power house becoming the continent's newest lootocracy?

[109] Kenya Advisor.com, the independent travel guide

[110] ibid

[111] Ibid John Githongo The Culture of Corruption in Kenya Presentation

[112]ibid

[113] ibid

[114] Ibid Peter Leftie pmutibo Hide and go seek with corruption. Daily Nation Dec. 17 2010

[115] John Githongo The Culture of Corruption in Kenya Presentation

[116] ibid

[117] ibid

[118] Michela Wrong Everyone Is Corrupt in Kenya, Even Grandmothers' Is East Africa's economic power house becoming the continent's newest lootocracy

[119] Peter Leftie pmutibo Hide and go seek with corruption. Daily Nation Dec. 17 2010

[120] Augustin Nguh CORRUPTION AND INFRASTRUCTURE MEGAPROJECTS IN THE DR CONGO A recipe for failure? Africa Program Research Fellow December

[121] wikipedia

[122] ibid

[123] Carter Dougherty War and corruption keep Congo tottering Published:New

York Times Thursday, September 2, 2004

[124] wikipedia

[125] ibid

[126] ibid

[127] Carter Dougherty War and corruption keep Congo tottering Published: New York times Thursday, September 2, 2004

[128] wikipedia

[129] ibid

[130] Nick Long/VOA News - May 14, 2012 Congo planet,

[131] ibid

[132] ibid

[133] ibid

Dean Peter Uvin Corruption and Violence in BurundiNew Routes Journal, No. 3 2009

ibid

Owei Lakemfa Wounded lion on the rampage vangaurd Nigeria May 22 2015

Dean Peter Uvin Corruption and Violence in BurundiNew Routes Journal, No. 3 2009

ibid

Country Reports on Human Rights Practices for 2012 United States Department of State Bureau of Democracy, Human Rights and Labor

Richard Grant, Paul Kagame: Rwanda's redeemer or ruthless dictator the telegraph 22 Jul 2010

The Robinson Library

Global Security.Org. Central African Republic –Francois Bozize

2015 Index Economic of economic freedom central African republic.

POLITICAL CORRUPTION IN SOUTH AFRICA Afr Aff (Lond) (1998) 97 (387):

South Africa reopens 1999 arms deal investigation

Stolen Assets Recovery Intiative: Jacob Zuma

ibid

Stoen Assests Recover Initiative: Thabo Mbeki

Ministry of foreign Affairs Denmark Business anti-corruption portal

DAVID E. MILLER THE MEDIA LINE \07/29/2010 The Jeruselem Post

[151] In the shade of Bourguiba: The Economist Nov 4th 2014

[152] Global security.org Military, Tunisa.

[153] International Journal of Economics And Management Sciences FACTORS INFLUENCING POLICE CORRUPTION IN LIBYA – A Preliminary Study. Omer M. Othman Domoro 1 and Syed Omar Syed Agil 2 1 Graduate School of Business, Universiti Tun Abdul Razak, Malaysia 2 Tun Abdul Razak School of Government, Universiti Tun Abdul Razak, Malaysia Vol. 2, No. 2, 2012, pp. 25-35

[154] Awa kalu: 50 years after Jan 1966: justice, order, rule of law Vangaurd 16 Jan 2016

[155] ibid

[156] ibid

[157] World Bank. (1997). Corruption. Retrieved from

[158] Ricky Munyaradzi Mukonza, Anti-corruption and Local Governance in Zimbabwe January 2013, Vol. 10, No. 1, 39-4

[159] Country Reports on Human Rights Practices for 2012 United States Department of State • Bureau of Democracy, Human Rights and Labor

[160] Sam K. Zinnah Sunday, January 24, 2010 The risk of impunity and Corruption in Liberia

[161] Richard Grant, Paul Kagame: Rwanda's redeemer or ruthless dictator the telegraph 22 Jul 2010

[162] ibid

[163] Emmanuel Dolo, Ph. D. & Winsley Nanka, CPA Tracking the Tentacles of Corruption: The Case of Liberia's Former Commerce Minister Samuel Wlue The perespective Atlanta, Georgia July 17, 2006

[164] Amara M. Konneh Minister of Planning & Economic Affairs Economic Crimes, Corruption and the Conflict in Liberia: Policy Options for an Emerging Democracy and sustainable Peace The Perspective Atlanta, Georgia February 24, 2009

[166] Anthony Akinola. Society and the corrupt power elite September 15, 2015

[167] Jehovah's Witnesses.org Jan 2015

[168] Arthur Kobina Kennedy - Ghanaian Chronicle Corruption in Ghana, 30 September 2009

[169] Ministry of foreign Affiars Danmark business anti corruption portal

[170] Obasanjo Olusegun :My Watch: Now and Then p 224

[171] Awo's thoughts: the new Dispensation : the rape on democracy of 1979, Tribune Newspaper

[172] Defeating the Islamic State: A Financial Military Strategy; Paul R. Khan

[173] Anti corruption resource center, Zambia

[174] Olusegun Obasanjo open letter to the Nigerian National Assembly

[175] BY GABRIEL ENOGHOLASE .vanguard how-we-ended-reign-of-terror-in-benin-city-without-bloodshed-ex-milad-oyakhire

[176] Ricky Munyaradzi Mukonza, Anti-corruption and Local Governance in Zimbabwe January 2013, Vol. 10, No. 1, 39-48

www.ingramcontent.com/pod-product-compliance
Lightning Source LLC
Chambersburg PA
CBHW070706290526
45790CB00001B/476

* 9 7 8 1 4 8 0 9 4 1 5 5 7 *